Chinese

KITCHEN

Chinese
KITCHEN

Linda Doeser

HERMES
HOUSE

This edition published in 2001 by Hermes House

© Anness Publishing Limited 1997, 2001

Published in the USA by Hermes House
Anness Publishing Inc.
27 West 20th Street
New York
NY 10011

Hermes House is an imprint of Anness Publishing Inc.

PUBLISHER: Joanna Lorenz
PROJECT EDITOR: Linda Doeser
COPY EDITOR: Harriette Lanzer
DESIGNER: Ian Sandom
PHOTOGRAPHY: Karl Adamson, Edward Allwright, David Armstrong, Steve Baxter, James Duncan, Michelle Garrett,
Amanda Heywood, Patrick McLeavy, Michael Michaels and Thomas Odulate
STYLING: Madeleine Brehaut, Michelle Garratt, Maria Kelly, Blake Minton and Kirsty Rawlings
FOOD FOR PHOTOGRAPHY: Carla Capalbo, Kit Chan, Elizabeth Wolf-Cohen, Joanne Craig, Nicola Fowler, Carole Handslip,
Jane Hartshorn, Shehzad Husain, Wendy Lee, Lucy McKelvie, Annie Nichols, Jane Stevenson and Steven Wheeler
ILLUSTRATIONS: Madeleine David
PRODUCTION CONTROLLER: Don Campaniello

Previously published as Best-ever Chinese and Asian

1 3 5 7 9 10 8 6 4 2

NOTES

Standard Spoon and cup measures are level.
Large eggs are used unless otherwise stated.

CONTENTS

INTRODUCTION

Chinese and other Asian food are increasingly popular in the West; our hunger for greater experience of these cuisines continues unabated. This book, with its extensive and wide-ranging collection of recipes, goes a long way toward appeasing the appetite for new gastronomic discoveries.

From the simple and familiar, such as Spring Rolls with Sweet Chili Dipping Sauce, to the more elaborate and unusual, like Lion's Head Casserole, there is something here to attract every cook. Stunning appetizers, including Mock Shark's Fin Soup and Lacy Duck Egg Nets, fabulous fish and seafood dishes, like Doedoeh of Fish, and mouthwatering meat and poultry, such as Paper-thin Lamb with Scallions and Chicken Teriyaki, are all here. The vibrant vegetable dishes include Chinese Potatoes with Chili Beans and Spiced Tofu Stir-fry, and there are sensational salads such as Sweet-and-Sour Fruit and Vegetable Salad. Noodle and rice recipes each have a section to themselves, and desserts are represented by such delights as Mango with Sticky Rice and Thai Coconut Custard.

Every recipe is temptingly illustrated with a full-color photograph of the finished dish, and clear step-by-step instructions and photographs show you how to achieve this end result. Additional guidance is provided by the sections on ingredients, techniques and equipment.

With its heavy reliance on wok cooking and fresh ingredients, Asian food is fast and nutritious as well as gastronomically and visually stimulating. A feast of exotic flavors is waiting to burst from the pages of this book into a kitchen near you.

INGREDIENTS

Bamboo shoots Mild-flavored, tender shoots of the young bamboo, widely available fresh, or sliced or halved in cans.

Basil Several different types of basil are used in Asian cooking. Thai cooks use two varieties, holy and sweet basil, but ordinary basil works well.

Bean curd See under Tofu.

Bean sprouts Shoots of the mung bean, usually available from supermarkets. They add a crisp texture to stir-fries.

Black bean sauce Made of salted black beans crushed and mixed with flour and spices (such as ginger, garlic or chili) to make a thick mixture. It is sold in cans and, once opened, should be kept in the refrigerator.

Bok choy Also known as Pak choi, this is a leaf vegetable with long, smooth, milky white stems and dark green foliage.

Cardamom pods Available both as small green pods and as larger black pods containing seeds, they have a strong aromatic quality.

Cashews Whole cashews feature prominently in Chinese stir-fries, especially those with chicken.

Cassia bark A form of cinnamon, but with a more robust flavor.

Chili bean sauce Made from fermented bean paste mixed with hot chili and other seasonings. Sold in jars, chili bean sauces are quite mild, but some are very hot.

Chili oil Made from dried red chilies, garlic, onions, salt and vegetable oil, this is used more as a dip than as a cooking ingredient.

Chili sauce A very hot sauce made from chilies, vinegar, sugar and salt. Usually sold in bottles, it should be used sparingly. Tabasco sauce can be a substitute.

Chilies There is a wide range of fresh and dried chilies from which to choose. Generally, the larger the chili, the milder the flavor, but there are some exceptions, and the only way to gauge potency is by taste. Remove the seeds for a milder flavor. Whether using dried or fresh chilies, take care when preparing them, as their seeds and flesh can "burn": wash your hands immediately afterward or, better still, wear rubber gloves—and never rub your eyes.

Chinese cabbage Also known as Chinese leaves, two types are widely available. The most commonly seen variety has a pale green color and tightly wrapped elongated head, and about two-thirds of the cabbage is cream, which has a crunchy texture. The other type has a shorter and fatter head with curlier, pale yellow or green leaves, and white stems.

Chinese chives Better known as garlic chives, these are sometimes sold with their flowers.

Chinese five-spice powder This flavoring contains star anise, pepper, fennel, cloves and cinnamon.

Chinese pancakes Thin flour-and-water pancakes with no added seasonings or spices. They are available fresh or frozen.

Chinese rice wine Made from glutinous rice, this is also known as yellow wine— *huang jin* or *chiew*—because of its color. The best variety is called Shao Hsing or Shaoxing and comes from the southeast of China. Dry sherry may be used as a substitute.

Coconut milk and cream Coconut milk should not be confused with the "milk" or juice found inside a fresh coconut (though the latter makes a refreshing drink). The coconut milk used for cooking is produced from the white flesh of the nut. If left to stand, the thick part of the milk will rise to the surface like cream.

To make your own, break open a fresh coconut and remove the brown inner skin from the flesh. Grate sufficient flesh to measure $1\frac{2}{3}$ cups. Place the grated flesh, together with $1\frac{1}{4}$ cups water, in a blender or food processor fitted with a metal blade and process for 1 minute. Strain the mixture through a strainer lined with cheesecloth into a bowl. Gather up the corners of the cheesecloth and squeeze out the liquid. The coconut milk is then ready to use, but you should stir it before use.

Coconut milk is also available in can.

Coriander Fresh coriander (cilantro) has a strong, pungent smell that combines well with other rich flavors. The white coriander root is used when the green coloring is not required. The seeds are also used, whole and ground.

Cornstarch paste To make cornstarch paste, mix 4 parts cornstarch with about 5 parts cold water until smooth.

Cumin Available as whole seeds and as a powder, cumin has a strong, slightly bitter flavor. It is used mainly in Indian recipes and in many other Asian dishes as well.

Curry paste Curry paste is traditionally made by pounding fresh herbs and spices in a mortar with a pestle. The two types of Thai curry paste, red and green, are made with red and green chilies, respectively. Other ingredients vary with individual cooks, but red curry paste typically contains ginger, shallots, garlic, coriander and cumin seeds and lime juice, as well as chilies. Herbs and flavorings in green curry paste usually include scallions, fresh cilantro, kaffir lime leaves, ginger, garlic and lemongrass. Making curry paste is time-consuming, but it tastes excellent and keeps well. Ready-made pastes, available in jars, are satisfactory substitutes.

Top shelf, left to right: *garlic, ginger, lemongrass, dried shrimp, Thai fish sauce, Szechuan peppercorns, sweet chili sauce, ground coriander, galangal, Chinese five-spice powder, fresh green chilies*
Middle shelf: *dried red chilies, peanuts (skins on), cardamom pods, cashew nuts (in jar), peanuts (skins off), kaffir lime leaves, tamarind, hoisin sauce, salted black beans, chili oil*
Bottom shelf, back row: *sake, rice vinegar, Chinese rice wine*
Bottom shelf, middle row: *sesame oil, mirin, peanut oil, fresh cilantro, cumin seeds*
Bottom shelf, front row: *basil, dried shrimp paste, red and green chilies, flaked coconut and creamed coconut, light soy sauce, oyster sauce, pieces of coconut, whole coconut*

Hoisin sauce A thick, dark brownish-red sauce that is sweet and spicy.

Kaffir lime leaves These are used rather like bay leaves, but to give an aromatic lime flavor to dishes. The fresh leaves are available from Asian food stores and can be frozen for future use.

Lemongrass Also known as citronella, lemongrass has a long, pale green stalk and a bulbous end similar to that of a scallion. Only the bottom five inches are used. It has a woody texture and an aromatic, lemony scent. Unless finely chopped, it is always removed before serving because it is so fibrous.

Lengkuas See under Galangal.

Mirin A mild, sweet Japanese rice wine used in cooking.

Miso A fermented bean paste that adds richness and flavor to Japanese soups.

Mushrooms Chinese shiitake mushrooms are used both fresh and dried to add texture and flavor to a dish. Wood ears are used in their dried form. All varieties of dried mushrooms need to be soaked in warm water for before use. Dried mushrooms are expensive, but a small quantity goes a long way.

Daikon A member of the radish family with a fresh, slightly peppery taste and white skin and flesh. Unlike other radishes, it is good when cooked, but should be salted and allowed to drain first, as it has a high water content. It is widely used in Chinese cooking and may be carved into an elaborate garnish.

Dashi Light Japanese broth, available in powder form. The flavor derives from kelp. Diluted vegetable broth made from a cube may be substituted.

Dried shrimp and shrimp paste Dried shrimp are tiny shrimp that are salted and dried. They are used as a seasoning for stir-fried dishes. First soak them in warm water until soft, then either process them in a blender or food processor or pound them in a mortar with a pestle. Shrimp paste, also known as *terasi*, is a dark, odorous paste made from fermented shrimp. Use sparingly.

Fish sauce The most commonly used flavoring in Thai food. Fish sauce (*nam pla*) is used in Thai cooking in the same way that soy sauce is used in Chinese dishes. It is made from salted anchovies and has a strong, salty flavor.

Galangal Fresh galangal, also known as *lengkuas*, tastes and looks a little like ginger with a pinkish tinge to its skin. Prepare it in the same way. It is also available dried and ground.

Garlic Garlic, together with ginger, is an indispensable ingredient in Asian cooking.

Ginger Fresh ginger has a sharp, distinctive flavor. Choose firm, plump pieces of fresh root with unwrinkled, shiny skins.

Gram flour Made from ground chickpeas, this flour has a unique flavor and is worth seeking out in Indian food stores.

Noodles: Cellophane noodles, also known as bean thread, transparent or glass noodles, are made from ground mung beans. Dried noodles must be soaked in hot water before cooking.

Egg noodles are made from wheat flour, egg and water. The dough is flattened and then shredded or extruded through a pasta machine to the required shape and thickness.

Rice noodles are made from ground rice and water. They range in thickness from very thin to wide ribbons and sheets. Dried ribbon rice noodles are usually sold tied together in bundles. Fresh rice noodles are also available. Rinse rice noodles in warm water and drain before use.

Rice vermicelli are thin, brittle noodles that look like white hair and are sold in large bundles. They cook almost instantly in hot liquid, provided the noodles are first soaked in warm water. They can also be deep-fried.

Somen noodles are delicate, thin, white Japanese noodles made from wheat flour. They are sold dried, usually tied in bundles held together with a paper band.

Udon noodles, also Japanese, are made of wheat flour and water. They are usually round but can also be flat and are available fresh, precooked or dried.

Nori Paper-thin sheets of Japanese seaweed.

Oyster sauce Made from oyster extract, this is used in many Asian fish dishes, soups and sauces.

Palm sugar Strongly flavored, hard brown sugar made from the sap of the coconut palm tree. It is available in Asian stores. If you have trouble finding it, use dark brown sugar instead.

Dried noodles, pictured

1 ribbon noodles	*7 cellophane noodles*
2 somen noodles	*8 rice sheets*
3 udon noodles	*9 rice vermicelli*
4 soba noodles	*10 egg noodles*
5 egg ribbon noodles	*11 rice ribbon noodles*
6 medium egg noodles	

Peanut oil This oil can be heated to a high temperature, making it perfect for stir-frying and deep-frying.

Peanuts Used to add flavor and a crunchy texture. The thin red skins must be removed before cooking: Immerse the peanuts in boiling water for a few minutes and then rub off the skins.

Red bean paste A reddish-brown paste made from puréed red beans and crystallized sugar. It is sold in cans.

Rice Long-grain rice is generally used for savory dishes. There are many high-quality varieties, coming from a range of countries. Basmati, which means "fragrant" in Hindi, is generally acknowledged as the king of rices. Thai jasmine rice is also fragrant and slightly sticky.

Rice vinegar There are two basic types of rice vinegar: Red vinegar is made from fermented rice and has a distinctive dark color and depth of flavor; white vinegar is stronger in flavor, as it is distilled from rice. If rice vinegar is unavailable, cider vinegar may be substituted.

Sake A strong, fortified rice wine from Japan.

Sesame oil This is used more for flavoring than for cooking. It is very intensely flavored, so only a little is required.

Soy sauce A major seasoning ingredient in Asian cooking, this is made from fermented soy beans combined with yeast, salt and sugar. Chinese soy sauce falls into two main categories: light and dark. Light soy sauce has more flavor than the sweeter dark soy sauce, which gives food a rich, reddish color.

Spring roll wrappers Paper-thin wrappers made from wheat or rice flour and water. Wheat wrappers are usually sold frozen and should be thawed and separated before use. Rice flour wrappers are dry and must be soaked before use.

Sweet potato The sweet richness of this red tuber marries well with the hot-and-sour flavors of Southeast Asia. In Japan the sweet potato is used to make delicious candies and sweetmeats.

Szechuan peppercorns Also known as *farchiew*, these aromatic red peppercorns are best used roasted and ground. They are not as hot as either white or black peppercorns, but do add a unique taste.

Tamari Japanese dark soy sauce with a mellow flavour. It is not so strong or concentrated as Chinese soy sauce.

Tamarind The brown, sticky pulp of the beanlike seedpod of the tamarind tree. It is used in Thai and Indonesian cooking to add tartness to recipes, much as Western cooks use vinegar or lemon juice. It is usually sold dried or pulped. The pulp is diluted with water and strained before use. Soak 1 ounce tamarind pulp in ⅔ cup warm water for about 10 minutes. Squeeze out as much tamarind juice as possible by pressing all the liquid through a strainer.

Terasi See under Dried Shrimp and shrimp paste.

Tofu This custardlike preparation of puréed and pressed soybeans, also known as bean curd, is high in protein. Plain tofu is bland in flavor but readily

absorbs the flavors of the food with which it is cooked. Tofu is also available smoked and marinated. Firm blocks of tofu are best suited to stir-frying.

Turmeric A member of the ginger family, turmeric is a rich, golden-colored root. If you are using the fresh root, wear rubber gloves when peeling it to avoid staining your skin. Turmeric is also available in powder form.

Wasabi This is an edible root that is used in Japanese cooking to make a condiment with a sharp, pungent and fiery flavor. It is very similar to horseradish and is available fresh, and in powder and paste form.

Water chestnuts Walnut-sized bulbs from an Asian water plant that look like sweet chestnuts. They are sold fresh by some Asian food stores, but are more readily available canned.

Top shelf, left to right: *fresh egg noodles, wonton wrappers, water chestnuts, cellophane noodles, gram flour, spring roll wrappers*
Middle shelf: *dried Chinese mushrooms, bok choy, tofu, dried egg noodles, Chinese pancakes*
Bottom shelf, at back: *rice; snow peas, baby corn, shallots, shiitake mushrooms (in basket); Chinese cabbage, rice vermicelli*
Bottom shelf, at front: *bamboo shoots, bean sprouts, wood ears (mushrooms), scallions, yard-long beans*

Wonton wrappers Small, paper-thin squares of wheat flour and egg dough.

Yard-long beans Long, thin beans similar to French beans but three or four times longer. Cut into smaller lengths and use just like ordinary green beans.

Yellow bean sauce A thick paste made from salted, fermented yellow soy beans, crushed with flour and sugar.

EQUIPMENT

You don't need special equipment to produce a Chinese or other Asian meal—you can even use a heavy-bottomed frying pan instead of a wok in many instances. However, the items listed below will make your Asian dishes easier and more pleasant to prepare.

Wok There are many different varieties of wok available. All are bowl-shaped, with gently sloping sides that allow the heat to spread rapidly and evenly over the surface. One that is about 14 inches in diameter is a useful size for most families, allowing adequate room for deep-frying, steaming and braising, as well as stir-frying.

Originally always made from cast iron, woks are now manufactured in a number of different metals. Cast iron remains very popular, as it is an excellent conductor of heat and develops a patina over a period of time that makes it virtually nonstick. Carbon steel is also a good choice, but stainless steel tends to scorch. Nonstick woks are available but are not really very efficient because they cannot withstand the high heat required for wok cooking. They are also expensive.

Woks may have an ear-shaped handle or two made from metal or wood, a single long handle or both. Wooden handles are safer.

Seasoning the wok New woks, apart from those with a nonstick lining, must be seasoned. Many need to be scrubbed first with a nonabrasive cleanser to remove the manufacturer's protective coating of oil. Once the oil has been removed, place the wok over low heat and add about 2 tablespoons vegetable oil. Rub the oil over the inside surface of the wok with a pad of paper towels. Heat the wok slowly for 10–15 minutes, then wipe off the oil with more paper towels. The paper will become black. Repeat this process of coating, heating and wiping several times until the paper comes out clean. Once the wok has been seasoned, it should not be scrubbed again. After use, just wash it in hot water without using any detergent, then wipe it completely dry before storage.

Wok accessories There is a range of accessories available to go with woks, but they are by no means essential.

Lid This is a useful addition, particularly if you want to use the wok for steaming and braising, as well as frying. Usually made of aluminum, it is a close-fitting, dome-shaped cover. Some woks are sold already supplied with matching lids. However, any snug-fitting, dome-shaped saucepan lid is an adequate substitute.

Stand This provides a secure base for the wok when it is used for steaming, braising or deep-frying and is a particularly useful accessory. Stands are always made of metal but vary in form, usually either a simple open-sided frame or a solid metal ring with holes punched around the sides.

Trivet This is essential for steaming to support the plate above the water level. Trivets are made of wood or metal.

Scoop This is a long-handled metal spatula, often with a wooden handle, used to toss ingredients during stir-frying. Any good, long-handled spoon can be used instead, although it does not have quite the same action.

Bamboo steamer This fits inside the wok, where it should rest safely perched on the sloping sides. Bamboo steamers range in size from small for dumplings and dim sum to those large enough to hold a whole fish.

Bamboo strainer This wide, flat metal strainer with a long bamboo handle makes lifting foods from steam or hot oil easier. A slotted metal spoon can also be used.

Other equipment Most equipment required for cooking the recipes in this book will be found in any kitchen. However, specialized tools are generally simple and inexpensive, especially if you seek out authentic implements from Asian stores.

A selection of cooking utensils, clockwise from top: *bamboo steamer, mortar and pestle, cutting board with cleaver, chef's knife and small paring knife, wok with lid and draining wire, wok scoop*

Cleaver No Chinese cook would be without one. This is an all-purpose cutting tool, available in various weights and sizes. It is easy to use and serves many purposes, from chopping up bones to precision cutting, such as deveining shrimp. It is a superb instrument for slicing vegetables thinly. It must be kept very sharp.

Mortar and pestle Usually made of earthenware or stone, this is extremely useful for grinding small amounts of spices and for pounding ingredients together to make pastes.

Food processor This is a quick and easy alternative to the mortar and pestle for grinding spices and making pastes. It can also be used for chopping and slicing vegetables.

COOKING TECHNIQUES

STIR-FRYING

This quick technique preserves the fresh flavor, color and texture of ingredients. Its success depends upon having everything you will need ready before starting to cook.

1 Heat an empty wok over high heat. This prevents food from sticking and will ensure an even heat. Add the oil and swirl it around so that it coats the base and halfway up the sides of the wok. It is important that the oil is hot when the food is added, so that it will start to cook immediately.

2 Add the ingredients in the order specified in the recipe. Aromatics (garlic, ginger, scallions) are usually added first: Do not wait for the oil to get so hot that it is almost smoking or they will burn and become bitter. Toss them in the oil for a few seconds. Next add the main ingredients that require longer cooking, such as dense vegetables or meat. Follow with the faster-cooking items. Toss the ingredients from the center of the wok to the sides using a wok scoop, long-handled spoon, or wooden spatula.

DEEP-FRYING

A wok is ideal for deep-frying, as it uses far less oil than a deep-fat fryer. Make sure that it is fully secure on its stand before adding the oil, and never leave the wok unattended.

1 Put the wok on a stand and half-fill with oil. Heat until the required temperature registers on a thermometer. Alternatively, test it by dropping in a small piece of food: If bubbles form all over the surface of the food, the oil is ready.

2 Carefully add the food to the oil using long wooden chopsticks or tongs, and move it around to prevent it from sticking. Use a wok scoop or slotted spoon to remove the food. Drain on paper towels before serving.

STEAMING

Steamed foods are cooked by a gentle moist heat, which must circulate freely in order for the food to cook. Steaming is increasingly popular with health-conscious cooks, as it preserves flavor and nutrients. It is perfect for vegetables, meat, poultry, and especially fish. The easiest way to steam food in a wok is by using a bamboo steamer.

USING A BAMBOO STEAMER

1 Put the wok on a stand. Pour in sufficient boiling water to come about 2 inches up the sides and bring back to the simmering point. Carefully put the bamboo steamer into the wok so that it rests securely against the sloping sides without touching the surface of the water.

2 Cover the steamer with its matching lid and cook for the time recommended in the recipe. Check the water level from time to time and add more boiling water if necessary.

USING A WOK AS A STEAMER

Put a trivet in the wok, then place the wok securely on its stand. Pour in sufficient boiling water to come just below the trivet. Carefully place a plate containing the food to be steamed on the trivet. Cover the wok with its lid, bring the water back to a boil, then lower the heat so that it is simmering gently. Steam for the time recommended in the recipe. Check the water level from time to time and add more boiling water if necessary.

SOUPS AND APPETIZERS

The delicious soups in this chapter can be served as a first course or as part of a selection of main course dishes, as they do in China. The recipes even include an unusual and satisfying Japanese breakfast soup. Many of the mouthwatering appetizers—a variety of spring rolls with spicy dipping sauces, dim sum, wontons and tempura—need no introduction, as they are long-established favorites in the West. Others are less well known, but just as tasty. Try Lacy Duck Egg Nets from Thailand or Spicy Meat Patties with Coconut from Indonesia, for example.

Basic Broth

This broth is used not only as the basis for soup making, but also for general cooking whenever liquid is required instead of plain water.

INGREDIENTS

Makes 10½ cups

1½ pounds chicken parts, skinned
1½ pounds pork spareribs
15 cups cold water
3–4 scallions, each tied into a knot
3–4 pieces fresh ginger, unpeeled and crushed
3–4 tablespoons Chinese rice wine or dry sherry

1 Trim off any excess fat from the chicken and spareribs and chop them into large pieces.

2 Place the chicken, spareribs and water in a large saucepan. Add the scallion knots and ginger.

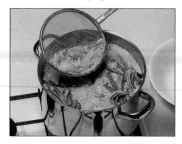

3 Bring to a boil and, using a strainer, skim off the foam. Reduce the heat and simmer, uncovered, for 2–3 hours.

4 Strain the broth, discarding the chicken, pork, scallions and ginger, and return it to the pan. Add the rice wine or dry sherry and bring to a boil. Simmer for 2–3 minutes. Refrigerate the broth when cool. It will keep for up to 5 days. Alternatively, it can be frozen in small containers and defrosted when required.

Chicken Wonton Soup with Shrimp

This soup is a more luxurious version of the familiar, basic wonton soup and is almost a meal in itself.

INGREDIENTS

Serves 4

10 ounces boneless chicken
  breast, skinned
7 ounces jumbo shrimp, raw or cooked
1 teaspoon finely chopped fresh ginger
2 scallions, finely chopped
1 egg
2 teaspoons oyster sauce (optional)
1 packet wonton wrappers
1 tablespoon cornstarch paste
3¾ cups chicken broth
¼ cucumber, peeled and diced
salt and freshly ground black pepper
1 scallion, cut into strips
4 sprigs fresh cilantro and 1 tomato,
  skinned, seeded and diced, to garnish

1 Place the chicken breast, three-quarters of the shrimp, the ginger and scallions in a food processor and process for 2–3 minutes. Add the egg, oyster sauce, if using, and seasoning and process briefly. Set aside.

2 Place 8 wonton wrappers at a time on a surface, moisten the edges with cornstarch paste and place ½ teaspoon of the chicken mixture in the center of each. Fold them in half and pinch to seal. Simmer in salted water for 4 minutes.

3 Bring the chicken broth to a boil, add the remaining shrimp and the cucumber and simmer for 3–4 minutes. Add the filled wontons and simmer for 3–4 minutes to warm through. Garnish with the scallion, cilantro and diced tomato and serve hot.

Thai Chicken Soup

The subtle combination of herbs, spices and creamed coconut makes this satisfying soup a special treat.

INGREDIENTS

Serves 4

1 tablespoon vegetable oil
1 garlic clove, finely chopped
2 boneless chicken breasts
   (6 ounces each), skinned and chopped
½ teaspoon ground turmeric
¼ teaspoon hot chili powder
3 ounces creamed coconut
3¾ cups hot chicken broth
2 tablespoons lemon or lime juice
2 tablespoons crunchy peanut butter
12 ounces thread egg noodles, broken
   into small pieces
1 tablespoon finely chopped scallion
1 tablespoon chopped fresh cilantro
salt and freshly ground black pepper
2 tablespoons shredded coconut and
   ½ fresh red chili, seeded and finely
   chopped, to garnish

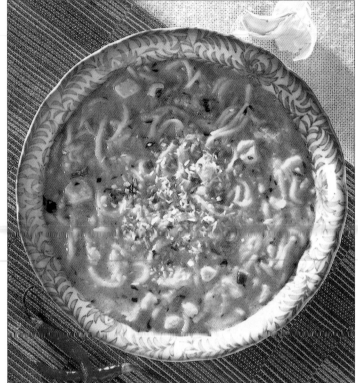

1 Heat the oil in a large pan and fry the garlic for 1 minute or until lightly golden. Add the chicken, turmeric and chili powder and stir-fry for another 3–4 minutes. Remove from heat.

2 Crumble the creamed coconut into the hot chicken broth and stir until dissolved. Pour into the pan with the chicken and add the lemon or lime juice, peanut butter and egg noodles.

3 Cover and simmer for about 15 minutes. Add the scallion and cilantro, then season well and cook for another 5 minutes.

4 Meanwhile, place the shredded coconut and chopped chili in a small frying pan and heat for 2–3 minutes, stirring frequently, until the coconut is lightly browned.

5 Serve the soup in bowls sprinkled with the fried coconut and chili.

Chinese Tofu and Lettuce Soup

This light, clear soup is brimful of nourishing, tasty vegetables.

INGREDIENTS

Serves 4

2 tablespoons peanut or sunflower oil
7 ounces smoked or marinated
   firm tofu, cubed
3 scallions, sliced diagonally
2 garlic cloves, cut into thin strips
1 carrot, thinly sliced into rounds
4 cups vegetable broth
2 tablespoons soy sauce
1 tablespoon dry sherry or vermouth
1 teaspoon sugar
4 ounces romaine lettuce, shredded
salt and freshly ground black pepper

1 Heat the oil in a preheated wok, then stir-fry the tofu until browned. Drain and set aside on paper towels.

2 Add the scallions, garlic and carrot to the wok and stir-fry for 2 minutes. Pour in the broth, soy sauce, dry sherry or vermouth, sugar and lettuce. Heat through gently for 1 minute, season to taste and serve hot.

Crab and Egg Noodle Broth

This delicious broth is the ideal solution when you are hungry, time is short and you need a fast, nutritious and filling meal.

INGREDIENTS

Serves 4

3 ounces thin egg noodles
2 tablespoons unsalted butter
1 small bunch scallions, chopped
1 celery stalk, sliced
1 medium carrot, cut into sticks
5 cups chicken broth
4 tablespoons dry sherry
4 ounces white crabmeat, fresh or
    frozen
pinch of celery salt
pinch of cayenne pepper
2 teaspoons lemon juice
1 small bunch cilantro or flat-leaf
    parsley, roughly chopped, to garnish

1 Bring a large saucepan of salted water to a boil. Toss in the egg noodles and cook according to the instructions on the package. Cool under cold running water and leave immersed in water until required.

COOK'S TIP

Fresh and frozen crabmeat have a better flavor than canned crab, which tends to taste rather bland.

2 Heat the butter in another large pan, add the scallions, celery and carrot, cover and cook the vegetables over gentle heat for 3-4 minutes or until soft.

3 Add the chicken broth and dry sherry, bring to a boil and simmer for another 5 minutes.

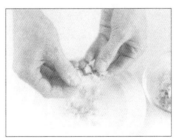

4 Flake the crabmeat between your fingers onto a plate and remove any stray pieces of shell.

5 Drain the noodles and add to the broth together with the crabmeat. Season to taste with celery salt and cayenne pepper and stir in the lemon juice. Return to a simmer.

6 Ladle the broth into shallow soup plates, scatter with roughly chopped cilantro or parsley and serve immediately.

Cheat's Shark's Fin Soup

Shark's fin soup is a renowned delicacy. In this poor man's vegetarian version, cellophane noodles, cut into short lengths, mimic shark's fin needles.

INGREDIENTS

Serves 4–6
4 dried Chinese mushrooms
1½ tablespoons dried wood ears
4 ounces cellophane noodles
2 tablespoons vegetable oil
2 carrots, cut into fine strips
4 ounces canned bamboo shoots,
  rinsed, drained and cut into
  fine strips
4 cups vegetable broth
1 tablespoon soy sauce
1 tablespoon arrowroot or potato flour
2 tablespoons water
1 egg white, beaten (optional)
1 teaspoon sesame oil
salt and freshly ground black pepper
2 scallions, finely chopped, to garnish
Chinese red vinegar, to serve (optional)

1 Soak the mushrooms and wood ears separately in warm water for 20 minutes. Drain well. Remove and discard the stems from the mushrooms and slice the caps thinly. Cut the wood ears into fine strips, discarding any hard pieces. Soak the noodles in hot water until soft. Drain and cut into short lengths. Set aside until required.

2 Heat the oil in a large saucepan. Add the mushrooms, and stir-fry for 2 minutes. Add the wood ears, stir-fry for 2 minutes, then stir in the carrots, bamboo shoots and noodles.

3 Add the broth to the pan. Bring to a boil, reduce the heat, and simmer gently for 15–20 minutes. Season with salt, pepper and soy sauce.

4 Blend the arrowroot or potato flour with a little water. Pour into the soup, stirring constantly to prevent lumps from forming as the soup continues to simmer.

5 Remove the pan from the heat. Stir in the egg white, if using, so that it sets to form small threads in the hot soup. Stir in the sesame oil, then pour the soup into individual bowls. Sprinkle each portion with chopped scallions, and offer the Chinese red vinegar separately, if using.

Miso Breakfast Soup

Miso is a fermented bean paste that adds richness and flavor to many of Japan's favorite soups. It is available in health food and specialty stores. This soup provides a nourishing start to the day.

INGREDIENTS

Serves 4

3 shiitake mushrooms, fresh or dried
5 cups vegetable broth
4 tablespoons miso paste
4 ounces firm tofu, cut into large dice
1 scallion, green part only, sliced, to garnish

1 If using dried mushrooms, soak them in hot water for 3–4 minutes, then drain. Slice the mushrooms thinly and set aside.

2 Bring the broth to a boil in a large saucepan. Stir in the miso paste and mushrooms, lower the heat, and simmer for 5 minutes.

3 Ladle the broth into four soup bowls and divide the tofu among them. Sprinkle the scallion on top and serve immediately.

Noodle Soup with Pork and Szechuan Pickle

INGREDIENTS

Serves 4

4 cups chicken broth
12 ounces egg noodles
1 tablespoon dried shrimp, soaked
   in water
2 tablespoons vegetable oil
8 ounces lean pork, finely shredded
1 tablespoon yellow bean paste
1 tablespoon soy sauce
4 ounces Szechuan hot pickle, rinsed,
   drained and shredded
pinch of sugar
salt and freshly ground black pepper
2 scallions, finely sliced, to garnish

1 Bring the broth to a boil in a large saucepan. Add the noodles, and cook until almost tender. Drain the dried shrimp, rinse under cold water, drain again, and add to the broth. Lower the heat, and simmer for about 2 minutes more. Keep hot. Heat the oil in a frying pan or wok. Add the pork, and stir-fry over a high heat for about 3 minutes.

2 Add the bean paste and soy sauce to the pork. Stir-fry for 1 minute more. Add the hot pickle with a pinch of sugar. Stir-fry for 1 minute more.

3 Divide the noodles and soup among individual serving bowls. Spoon the pork mixture on top, then sprinkle with the scallions. Serve the dish at once.

Snapper, Tomato and Tamarind Noodle Soup

Tamarind gives this light, fragrant noodle soup a slightly sour taste.

INGREDIENTS

Serves 4

8 cups water
2¼ pounds red snapper (or other red
   fish such as bass)
1 onion, sliced
2 ounces tamarind pods
1 tablespoon fish sauce
1 tablespoon sugar
2 tablespoons vegetable oil
2 garlic cloves, finely chopped
2 lemon grass stalks, very
   finely chopped
4 ripe tomatoes, coarsely chopped
2 tablespoons yellow bean paste
8 ounces rice vermicelli, soaked in
   warm water until soft
4 ounces bean sprouts
8–10 basil or mint sprigs
¼ cup roasted peanuts, ground
salt and freshly ground black pepper

1 Bring the water to a boil in a saucepan. Lower the heat, and add the fish and onion, with ½ teaspoon salt. Simmer gently until the fish is cooked right through.

2 Remove the fish from the stock, and set aside. Add the tamarind, fish sauce and sugar to the stock. Cook for 5 minutes, then strain the stock into a large pitcher or bowl. Carefully remove all of the bones from the fish, keeping the flesh in big pieces.

3 Heat the oil in a large frying pan. Add the garlic and lemon grass, and fry for a few seconds. Stir in the tomatoes and bean paste. Cook gently for 5–7 minutes, until the tomatoes are soft. Add the stock, bring back to a simmer, and adjust the seasoning.

4 Drain the vermicelli. Plunge it into a saucepan of boiling water for a few minutes, drain, and divide among individual serving bowls. Add the bean sprouts, fish, basil or mint, and sprinkle the ground peanuts on top. Fill each bowl with the hot soup.

Beef Noodle Soup

A steaming bowl, packed with delicious flavors and a taste of the Orient, will be welcome on cold winter days.

INGREDIENTS

Serves 4

¼ ounce dried porcini mushrooms
⅔ cup boiling water
6 scallions
2 medium carrots
12 ounces sirloin steak
about 2 tablespoons sunflower oil
1 garlic clove, crushed
1-inch piece fresh ginger, peeled and finely chopped
5 cups beef broth
3 tablespoons light soy sauce
4 tablespoons Chinese rice wine or dry sherry
3 ounces thin egg noodles
3 ounces spinach, shredded
salt and freshly ground black pepper

3 Heat the oil in a large saucepan and brown the beef in batches, adding a little more oil if necessary. Remove the beef with a slotted spoon and set aside to drain on paper towels.

4 Add the garlic, ginger, scallions and carrots to the pan and stir-fry for 3 minutes.

5 Add the beef broth, the mushrooms and their soaking liquid, the soy sauce, rice wine or dry sherry and plenty of seasoning. Bring to a boil and simmer, covered, for 10 minutes.

6 Break up the noodles slightly and add to the pan with the spinach. Simmer gently for 5 minutes, or until the beef is tender. Adjust the seasoning before serving.

1 Break the mushrooms into small pieces, place in a bowl and pour the boiling water over them. Set aside to soak for 15 minutes.

2 Shred the scallions and carrots into fine 2-inch-long strips. Trim any fat off the steak and slice into thin strips.

Pork and Noodle Broth with Shrimp

This delicately flavored Vietnamese soup is very quick and easy to make, but tastes really special.

INGREDIENTS

Serves 4–6

12 ounces pork chops or loins
8 ounces jumbo shrimp, raw or cooked
5 ounces thin egg noodles
1 tablespoon vegetable oil
2 teaspoons sesame oil
4 shallots or 1 medium onion, sliced
1 tablespoon finely sliced fresh
 ginger
1 garlic clove, crushed
1 teaspoon sugar
6¼ cups chicken broth
2 kaffir lime leaves
3 tablespoons fish sauce
juice of ½ lime
4 sprigs fresh cilantro and 2 scallions,
 green parts only, chopped,
 to garnish

1 If you are using pork chops, trim away any fat and the bones. Place the meat in the freezer for 30 minutes to firm, but not freeze it. Slice the pork thinly and set aside. Peel and devein the shrimp, if using raw shrimp.

2 Bring a large saucepan of salted water to a boil and simmer the noodles according to the instructions on the package. Drain and refresh in cold water. Set aside.

3 Heat the vegetable and sesame oils in a preheated wok, add the shallots or onion and stir-fry for 3–4 minutes, or until evenly browned. Remove from the wok and set aside.

4 Add the ginger, garlic, sugar and chicken broth to the wok and bring to a simmer. Add the lime leaves, fish sauce and lime juice. Add the pork, then simmer for 15 minutes. Add the shrimp and noodles and simmer for 3–4 minutes to heat through. Serve in shallow bowls, garnished with cilantro sprigs, the green parts of the scallions and the browned shallots or onion.

Hanoi Beef and Noodle Soup

Millions of North Vietnamese eat this fragrant soup for breakfast.

INGREDIENTS

Serves 4–6
1 onion
3–3½ pounds beef shank with bones
1 inch fresh ginger
1 star anise
1 bay leaf
2 whole cloves
½ teaspoon fennel seeds
1 piece of cassia bark or
    cinnamon stick
12 cups water
fish sauce, to taste
juice of 1 lime
5 ounces fillet steak
1 pound fresh flat rice noodles
salt and freshly ground black pepper

For the accompaniments
1 small red onion, sliced into rings
4 ounces bean sprouts
2 red chilies, seeded and sliced
2 scallions, finely sliced
handful of cilantro leaves

1 Cut the onion in half. Broil under a high heat, cut side up, until the exposed sides are caramelized, and deep brown. Set aside.

2 Cut the meat into large chunks, and then place with the bones in a large saucepan or stock pot. Add the caramelized onion with the ginger, star anise, bay leaf, cloves, fennel seeds and cassia bark or cinnamon stick.

3 Add the water, bring to a boil, reduce the heat, and simmer gently for 2–3 hours, skimming off the fat and scum from time to time.

4 Using a slotted spoon, remove the meat from the stock. When cool enough to handle, cut into small pieces, discarding the bones. Strain the stock, and return to the pan or stock pot together with the meat. Bring back to a boil, and season with the fish sauce and the lime juice.

5 Slice the fillet steak very thinly, and then chill until required. Place the accompaniments in separate bowls.

6 Cook the noodles in a large saucepan of boiling water until just tender. Drain, and divide among individual serving bowls. Arrange the thinly sliced steak over the noodles, and pour the hot stock on top. Serve, offering the accompaniments separately so that each person may garnish their soup as they like.

Tamarind Soup with Peanuts and Vegetables

Sayur Asam is a colorful and refreshing soup from Jakarta with more than a hint of sharpness.

INGREDIENTS

Serves 4 or 8 as part of a buffet
For the spice paste
5 shallots or 1 medium red
  onion, sliced
3 garlic cloves, crushed
1 inch *laos,* peeled and sliced
1–2 fresh red chilies, seeded and sliced
3 tablespoons raw peanuts
1 teaspoon shrimp paste
5 cups well-flavored chicken or
  vegetable broth
½ cup salted peanuts, lightly crushed
1–2 tablespoons dark brown sugar
1 teaspoon tamarind pulp, soaked in
  5 tablespoons warm water for
  15 minutes
salt

For the vegetables
1 chayote, thinly peeled, seeds
  removed, flesh finely sliced
4 ounces green beans, trimmed and
  finely sliced
⅓ cup corn kernels (optional)
handful green leaves, such as
  watercress, arugula or Chinese
  cabbage, finely shredded
1 fresh green chili, sliced, to garnish

1 Prepare the spice paste by grinding the shallots or onion, garlic, *laos,* chilies, raw peanuts and shrimp paste to a paste in a food processor or with a mortar and pestle.

2 Pour in some of the broth to moisten and then pour this mixture into a pan or wok, adding the rest of the broth. Cook for 15 minutes with the lightly crushed peanuts and sugar.

3 Strain the tamarind, discarding the seeds, and reserve the juice.

4 About 5 minutes before serving, add the chayote slices, beans and corn, if using, to the soup and cook fairly rapidly. At the last minute, add the greens or cabbage.

5 Add the tamarind juice and taste for seasoning. Serve, garnished with slices of green chili.

Shrimp Crackers

These are a popular addition to many Chinese and other Far Eastern dishes and are often served before guests come to the table. Freshly cooked shrimp crackers are more delicious than the ready-to-eat variety.

INGREDIENTS

Serves 4–6
1¼ cups vegetable oil
2 ounces uncooked shrimp crackers
salt, to serve

1 Line a tray with paper towels. Heat the oil in a large wok until it begins to smoke. Reduce the heat to maintain a steady temperature. Drop 3 or 4 shrimp crackers into the oil.

2 After they swell up, remove them from the oil almost immediately, before they start to color. Transfer to the paper-lined tray to drain. Serve sprinkled with salt.

Hot Chili Shrimp

These can be prepared up to eight hours in advance and are delicious either grilled or barbecued.

INGREDIENTS

Serves 4–6
1 garlic clove, crushed
½-inch piece fresh ginger, finely chopped
1 small fresh red chili, seeded and chopped
2 teaspoons sugar
1 tablespoon light soy sauce
1 tablespoon vegetable oil
1 teaspoon sesame oil
juice of 1 lime
1½ pounds jumbo shrimp
6 ounces cherry tomatoes
½ cucumber, cut into chunks
salt
1 small bunch cilantro, roughly chopped, to garnish
lettuce leaves, to serve

1 Pound the garlic, ginger, chili and sugar to a paste in a mortar with a pestle. Add the soy sauce, vegetable and sesame oils, lime juice and salt to taste. Place the shrimp in a shallow dish and pour the marinade over them. Set aside to marinate for up to 8 hours. Soak some bamboo skewers.

2 Thread the shrimp, tomatoes and cucumber chunks onto bamboo skewers. Cook under a preheated broiler or on a grill for 3–4 minutes. Transfer to a serving dish, scatter the cilantro on top, and serve on a bed of lettuce.

Spring Rolls with Sweet Chili Dipping Sauce

Miniature spring rolls make a delicious appetizer or unusual finger food for serving at a party.

INGREDIENTS

Makes 20–24
1 ounce rice vermicelli noodles
peanut oil, for deep-frying
1 teaspoon grated fresh ginger
2 scallions, cut into fine strips
1 medium carrot, cut into fine strips
2 ounces snow peas, cut into fine strips
1 ounce young spinach leaves
2 ounces fresh bean sprouts
1 tablespoon chopped fresh mint
1 tablespoon chopped fresh cilantro
2 tablespoons fish sauce
20–24 spring roll wrappers, each
   5 inches square
1 egg white, lightly beaten

For the dipping sauce
¼ cup superfine sugar
¼ cup rice vinegar
2 tablespoons water
2 fresh red chilies, seeded and finely
   chopped

1 First make the dipping sauce. Place the sugar, vinegar and water in a small pan. Heat gently, stirring until the sugar dissolves, then boil rapidly until it forms a light syrup. Stir in the chilies and let cool.

2 Soak the noodles according to the package instructions, then rinse and drain well. Using scissors, snip the noodles into short lengths.

3 Heat 1 tablespoon of the oil in a preheated wok and swirl it around. Add the ginger and scallions and stir-fry for 15 seconds. Add the carrot and snow peas and stir-fry for 2–3 minutes. Add the spinach, bean sprouts, mint, cilantro, fish sauce and noodles and stir-fry for another minute. Set aside to cool.

4 Soften the spring roll wrappers, following the directions on the package. Take one spring roll wrapper and arrange it so that it faces you in a diamond shape. Place a spoonful of filling just below the center, then fold up the bottom point over the filling.

5 Fold in each side, then roll up tightly. Brush the end with beaten egg white to seal. Repeat until all the filling has been used up.

6 Half-fill a wok with oil and heat to 350°F. Deep-fry the spring rolls in batches for 3–4 minutes or until golden and crisp. Drain on paper towels. Serve hot with the sweet chili dipping sauce.

COOK'S TIP

You can cook the spring rolls 2–3 hours in advance, then reheat them on a foil-lined baking sheet at 400°F for about 10 minutes.

Crab Spring Rolls and Dipping Sauce

Chili and grated ginger add a hint of heat to these sensational treats. Serve them as an appetizer or with other Chinese dishes as part of a main course.

INGREDIENTS

Serves 4–6

1 tablespoon peanut oil
1 teaspoon sesame oil
1 garlic clove, crushed
1 fresh red chili, seeded and finely sliced
1 pound fresh stir-fry vegetables, such as bean sprouts and shredded carrots, bell peppers and snow peas
2 tablespoons chopped cilantro
1-inch piece fresh ginger, grated
1 tablespoon Chinese rice wine or dry sherry
1 tablespoon soy sauce
12 ounces fresh dressed crabmeat (brown and white meat)
12 spring roll wrappers
1 small egg, beaten
oil, for deep-frying
salt and freshly ground black pepper
lime wedges and fresh cilantro, to garnish

For the dipping sauce

1 onion, thinly sliced
oil, for deep-frying
1 fresh red chili, seeded and finely chopped
2 garlic cloves, crushed
4 tablespoons dark soy sauce
4 teaspoons lemon juice or 1–1½ tablespoons prepared tamarind juice
2 tablespoons hot water

1 First make the sauce. Spread the onion out on paper towels and let dry for 30 minutes. Then half-fill a wok with oil and heat to 375°F. Fry the onion in batches until crisp and golden, turning all the time. Drain on paper towels.

2 Combine the chili, garlic, soy sauce, lemon or tamarind juice and hot water in a bowl.

3 Stir in the onion and let stand for 30 minutes.

4 To make the spring rolls, heat the peanut and sesame oils in a clean, preheated wok. When hot, stir-fry the crushed garlic and chili for 1 minute. Add the vegetables, cilantro and ginger and stir-fry for 1 minute more. Drizzle with the rice wine or dry sherry and soy sauce. Allow the mixture to bubble up for 1 minute.

5 Using a slotted spoon, transfer the vegetables to a bowl. Set aside until cool, then stir in the crabmeat and season with salt and pepper.

6 Soften the spring roll wrappers, following the directions on the package. Place some of the filling on a wrapper, fold over the front edge and the sides, and roll up neatly, sealing the edges with a little beaten egg. Repeat with the remaining wrappers and filling.

7 Heat the oil for deep-frying in the wok and fry the spring rolls in batches, turning several times, until brown and crisp. Remove with a slotted spoon, drain on paper towels and keep hot while frying the remainder. Serve at once, garnished with lime wedges and cilantro, with the dipping sauce.

Mini Spring Rolls

Eat these irresistibly light and crisp rolls with your fingers. If you like slightly spicier food, sprinkle them with a little cayenne pepper before serving.

INGREDIENTS

Makes 20

1 green chili
½ cup vegetable oil
1 small onion, finely chopped
1 garlic clove, crushed
3 ounces cooked boneless chicken breast, skinned
1 small carrot, cut into short thin sticks
1 scallion, finely sliced
1 small red bell pepper, seeded and cut into short thin sticks
1 ounce bean sprouts
1 teaspoon sesame oil
4 large sheets phyllo pastry
1 small egg white, lightly beaten
chives to garnish (optional)
3 tablespoons light soy sauce, to serve

1 Carefully remove the seeds from the chili and chop finely, wearing rubber gloves to protect your hands, if necessary.

2 Heat 2 tablespoons of the vegetable oil in a preheated wok. Add the onion, garlic and chili and stir-fry for 1 minute.

3 Slice the chicken breast very thinly, then add to the wok and fry over high heat, stirring constantly, until browned.

4 Add the carrot, scallion and red bell pepper and stir-fry for 2 minutes. Add the bean sprouts, stir in the sesame oil, and let cool.

5 Cut each sheet of phyllo pastry into 5 short strips. Place a small amount of filling at one end of each strip, then fold in the long sides and roll up the pastry. Seal and glaze the rolls with the egg white, then chill, uncovered, for 15 minutes before frying.

6 Wipe the wok with paper towels, reheat it, and add the remaining vegetable oil. When the oil is hot, fry the rolls in batches until crisp and golden brown. Drain on paper towels and serve, garnished with chives, if using, and dipped in light soy sauce.

COOK'S TIP

Be careful to avoid touching your face or eyes when seeding and chopping chilies, because they are very potent and may cause burning and irritation to the skin. Try preparing chilies under running water.

Crab, Pork and Mushroom Spring Rolls

If you cannot obtain ground pork, use the meat from the equivalent weight of best-quality pork sausages. Filled spring rolls can be made in advance and kept in the refrigerator until they are ready for frying.

INGREDIENTS

Serves 4–6

1 ounce rice noodles
2 ounces shiitake mushrooms, fresh or dried
vegetable oil, for deep-frying
4 scallions, chopped
1 small carrot, grated
6 ounces ground pork
4 ounces white crabmeat
1 teaspoon fish sauce (optional)
12 frozen spring roll wrappers, defrosted
2 tablespoons cornstarch paste
salt and ground black pepper
1 head iceberg or Bibb lettuce, separated into leaves
1 bunch fresh mint or basil, coarsely chopped
1 bunch fresh cilantro leaves, coarsely chopped
½ cucumber, sliced

1 Bring a large saucepan of salted water to a boil, add the noodles and simmer for 8 minutes. Cut the noodles into finger-length pieces. If the mushrooms are dried, soak them in hot water for 10 minutes, then drain. Slice the mushrooms thinly.

2 To make the filling, heat 1 tablespoon of the oil in a wok or frying pan, add the scallions, carrot and pork and cook for 8–10 minutes. Remove from the heat, then add the crabmeat, fish sauce, if using, and seasoning. Add the noodles and mushrooms and set aside.

3 To fill the rolls, brush one spring roll wrapper at a time with the cornstarch paste, then place 1 teaspoon of the filling on the skin. Fold the edges toward the middle and roll evenly to make a neat cigar shape. The paste will help seal the wrapper.

4 Heat the oil for deep-frying in a wok or deep-fryer until hot. Fry the spring rolls, two or three at a time, for 6–8 minutes. Make sure the oil is not too hot, or the filling will not heat through. Arrange the lettuce leaves, mint or basil, cilantro and cucumber on a serving platter and top with the spring rolls.

Dim Sum

Popular as a snack in China, these tiny dumplings are fast becoming fashionable in many restaurants in the West.

INGREDIENTS

Serves 4
For the dough
1¼ cups all-purpose flour
¼ cup boiling water
1½ tablespoons cold water
½ tablespoon vegetable oil

For the filling
3 ounces ground pork
3 tablespoons canned chopped
   bamboo shoots
1 tablespoon light soy sauce
1 teaspoon dry sherry
1 teaspoon light brown sugar
½ teaspoon sesame oil
1 teaspoon cornstarch
lettuce leaves such as iceberg or frisée,
   soy sauce, scallion curls, sliced fresh
   red chili and shrimp crackers,
   to serve

1 To make the dough, sift the flour into a bowl. Stir in the boiling water, then the cold water together with the oil. Mix to form a dough, turn out onto a lightly floured surface, and knead until smooth.

2 Divide the mixture into 16 equal pieces and shape into circles.

3 For the filling, mix together the pork, bamboo shoots, soy sauce, dry sherry, sugar and oil.

4 Add the cornstarch and stir well until thoroughly combined.

5 Place a little of the filling in the center of each dim sum circle. Pinch the edges of the dough together to form little "purses."

6 Line a steamer with a damp kitchen towel. Place the dim sum in the steamer and steam for 5–10 minutes. Arrange the lettuce leaves on four individual serving plates, top with the dim sum and serve with soy sauce, scallion curls, sliced red chili and shrimp crackers.

VARIATION

You can replace the pork with cooked, peeled shrimp. Sprinkle 1 tablespoon sesame seeds over the dim sum before cooking, if desired.

Crab and Tofu Dumplings

These little crab- and ginger-flavored dumplings are usually served as a delicious side dish as part of a Japanese meal.

Ingredients

Serves 4–6

4 ounces frozen white crabmeat, thawed
4 ounces firm tofu
1 egg yolk
2 tablespoons rice flour or wheat flour
2 tablespoons finely chopped scallion, green part only
¼-inch piece fresh ginger, grated
2 teaspoons light soy sauce
salt
vegetable oil, for deep-frying
2 ounces daikon, very finely grated, to serve

For the dipping sauce
½ cup vegetable broth
1 tablespoon sugar
3 tablespoons dark soy sauce

1 Squeeze as much moisture out of the crabmeat as you can. Press the tofu through a fine sieve with the back of a tablespoon. Combine the tofu and crabmeat in a bowl.

2 Add the egg yolk, rice or wheat flour, scallion, ginger and soy sauce and season to taste with salt. Combine thoroughly to form a light paste.

3 To make the dipping sauce, combine the broth, sugar and soy sauce in a serving bowl.

4 Line a tray with paper towels. Heat the vegetable oil in a wok or frying pan to 375°F. Meanwhile, shape the crab and tofu mixture into thumb-sized pieces. Fry in batches of three at a time for 1–2 minutes. Drain on the paper towels and serve with the sauce and daikon.

Steamed Pork and Water Chestnut Wontons

Ginger and Chinese five-spice powder flavor this version of steamed dumplings—a favorite snack in many teahouses.

INGREDIENTS

Makes about 36
2 large Chinese cabbage leaves, plus extra for lining the steamer
2 scallions, finely chopped
½-inch piece fresh ginger, chopped
2 ounces canned water chestnuts, rinsed and finely chopped
8 ounces ground pork
½ teaspoon Chinese five-spice powder
1 tablespoon cornstarch
1 tablespoon light soy sauce
1 tablespoon Chinese rice wine or dry sherry
2 teaspoons sesame oil
generous pinch of superfine sugar
about 36 wonton wrappers, each 3 inches square
light soy sauce and hot chili oil, for dipping

1 Place the Chinese cabbage leaves one on top of the other. Cut them lengthwise into quarters and then across into thin shreds.

2 Place the shredded Chinese cabbage leaves in a bowl. Add the scallions, ginger, water chestnuts, pork, five-spice powder, cornstarch, soy sauce, rice wine or dry sherry, sesame oil and sugar and mix well.

3 Place a heaped teaspoon of the filling in the center of a wrapper. Lightly dampen the edges with water.

4 Lift the wrapper up around the filling, gathering it to form a "purse." Squeeze the wrapper firmly around the middle, then tap the bottom to make a flat base. The top should be open. Place the wonton on a tray and cover with a damp kitchen towel. Repeat until the filling is used up.

5 Line a steamer with cabbage leaves and steam the dumplings for 12–15 minutes, or until tender. Remove each batch from the steamer as soon they are cooked, cover with foil and keep warm. Serve hot with soy sauce and chili oil for dipping.

Seafood Wontons with Cilantro Dressing

These tasty wontons resemble tortellini. Water chestnuts add a light crunch to the filling.

INGREDIENTS

Serves 4
8 ounces raw shrimp, peeled
  and deveined
4 ounces white crabmeat, picked over
4 canned water chestnuts, finely diced
1 scallion, finely chopped
1 small green chili, seeded and
  finely chopped
½ teaspoon grated fresh ginger
1 egg, separated
20–24 wonton wrappers
salt and freshly ground black pepper
cilantro leaves, to garnish

For the cilantro dressing
2 tablespoons rice vinegar
1 tablespoon chopped pickled ginger
6 tablespoons olive oil
1 tablespoon soy sauce
3 tablespoons chopped cilantro
2 tablespoons diced red bell pepper

1 Finely dice the shrimp, and place in a bowl. Add the crabmeat, water chestnuts, scallion, chili, ginger and egg white. Season with salt and pepper, and stir well.

2 Place a wonton wrapper on a board. Put about 1 teaspoon of the filling just above the center of the wrapper. With a pastry brush, moisten the edges of the wrapper with a little of the egg yolk. Bring the bottom of the wrapper up over the filling. Press gently to expel any air, then seal the wrapper neatly in a triangle.

3 For a more elaborate shape, bring the two side points up over the filling, overlap the points, and pinch the ends firmly together. Place the filled wontons on a large baking sheet, lined with wax paper, so that they do not stick together.

4 Half fill a large saucepan with water. Bring to simmering point. Add the filled wontons, a few at a time, and simmer for 2–3 minutes. The wontons will float to the surface. When ready, the wrappers will be translucent and the filling should be cooked. Remove the wontons with a large slotted spoon, drain them briefly, then spread them on trays. Keep warm while cooking the remaining wontons.

5 Make the cilantro dressing by whisking all the ingredients together in a bowl. Divide the wontons among serving dishes, drizzle with the dressing, and serve garnished with a handful of cilantro leaves.

Wonton Flowers with Sweet-and-Sour Sauce

These melt-in-the-mouth, crisp dumplings make a delicious first course or snack—and take hardly any time at all to prepare.

INGREDIENTS

Serves 4–6
16–20 wonton wrappers
vegetable oil, for deep-frying

For the sauce
1 tablespoon vegetable oil
2 tablespoons light brown sugar
3 tablespoons rice vinegar
1 tablespoon light soy sauce
1 tablespoon ketchup
3–4 tablespoons broth or water
1 tablespoon cornstarch paste

1 Pinch the center of each wonton wrapper and twist it around to form a floral shape.

2 Heat the oil in a wok and deep-fry the floral wontons for 1–2 minutes, until crisp. Remove and drain on paper towels.

3 To make the sauce, heat the oil in a wok or frying pan and add the sugar, vinegar, soy sauce, ketchup and broth or water.

4 Stir in the cornstarch paste to thicken the sauce. Continue stirring until smooth. Pour a little sauce over the wontons and serve immediately with the remaining sauce.

Seared Scallops with Wonton Crisps

Quick seared scallops with crisp
vegetables in a lightly spiced
sauce make a lovely appetizer.

INGREDIENTS

Serves 4
16 scallops, halved
oil for deep-frying
8 wonton wrappers
3 tablespoons olive oil
1 large carrot, cut into long thin strips
1 large leek, cut into long thin strips
juice of 1 lemon
juice of ½ orange
2 scallions, finely sliced
2 tablespoons cilantro leaves
salt and freshly ground black pepper

For the marinade
1 teaspoon Thai red curry paste
1 teaspoon grated fresh ginger
1 garlic clove, finely chopped
1 tablespoon soy sauce
1 tablespoon olive oil

1 Make the marinade by mixing all
the ingredients in a bowl. Add the
scallops, toss to coat, and let marinate
for about 30 minutes.

2 Heat the oil in a large heavy-
bottomed saucepan or deep-fryer,
and deep-fry the wonton wrappers in
small batches until crisp and golden.

3 When the wrappers are ready,
drain them on paper towels. Set
aside until required.

4 Heat half the olive oil in a large
frying pan. Add the scallops, with
the marinade, and sear over a high heat
for about 1 minute or until golden,
taking care not to overcook (they
should feel firm to the touch but not
rubbery). Using a slotted spoon,
transfer the scallops to a plate.

5 Add the remaining olive oil to the
pan. When hot, add the carrot and
leek strips. Toss and turn the vegetables
until they start to wilt and soften, but
remain crisp. Season to taste with salt
and pepper, stir in the lemon and
orange juices, and add a little more soy
sauce if needed.

6 Return the scallops to the pan, mix
lightly with the vegetables, and
heat for just long enough to warm
through. Transfer to a bowl, and add
the scallions and cilantro. To serve,
sandwich a quarter of the mixture
between two wonton crisps. Make
three more "sandwiches" in the same
way, and serve at once.

Rice Cakes with Spicy Dipping Sauce

Rice cakes are a classic Thai appetizer. They are easy to make and can be kept in an airtight box almost indefinitely.

INGREDIENTS

Serves 4–6
1 cup jasmine rice
1½ cups water
oil for frying and greasing

For the spicy dipping sauce
6–8 dried chilies
½ teaspoon salt
2 shallots, chopped
2 garlic cloves, chopped
4 cilantro roots
10 white peppercorns
1 cup unsweetened coconut milk
1 teaspoon shrimp paste
4 ounces ground pork
4 ounces cherry tomatoes, chopped
1 tablespoon fish sauce
1 tablespoon palm sugar
2 tablespoons tamarind juice
2 tablespoons coarsely chopped
   roasted peanuts
2 scallions, finely chopped

1 Stem the chilies and remove most of the seeds. Soak the chilies in warm water for 20 minutes. Drain and transfer to a mortar.

2 Add the salt and grind with a pestle until the chilies are crushed. Add the shallots, garlic, cilantro roots and peppercorns. Pound together until you have a coarse paste.

3 Pour the coconut milk into a saucepan and boil until it begins to separate. Add the pounded chili paste. Cook for 2–3 minutes, until it is fragrant. Stir in the shrimp paste. Cook for another minute.

4 Add the pork, stirring to break up any lumps. Cook for about 5–10 minutes. Add the tomatoes, fish sauce, palm sugar and tamarind juice. Simmer until the sauce thickens.

5 Stir in the chopped peanuts and scallions. Remove from the heat and set aside to cool.

6 Wash the rice in several changes of water. Put in a saucepan, add the water and cover with a tight-fitting lid. Bring to a boil, reduce the heat and simmer gently for about 15 minutes.

7 Remove the lid and fluff up the rice. Turn out on to a lightly greased tray and press down with the back of a large spoon. Set aside to dry out overnight in a very low oven, until it is completely dry and firm.

8 Remove the rice from the tray and break into bite-size pieces. Heat the oil in a wok or deep-fat fryer.

9 Deep-fry the rice cakes in batches for about 1 minute, until they puff up, taking care not to brown them too much. Remove and drain. Serve accompanied with the dipping sauce.

Vegetable Tempura

These deep-fried fritters are based on *kaki-age*, a Japanese dish that often incorporates fish and shrimp as well as vegetables.

INGREDIENTS

Serves 4

2 medium zucchini
½ medium eggplant
1 large carrot
½ small Spanish onion
1 egg
½ cup ice water
1 cup all-purpose flour
salt and ground black pepper
vegetable oil, for deep-frying
sea salt flakes, lemon slices and Japanese
soy sauce (*shoyu*), to serve

1 Using a potato peeler, pare strips of peel from the zucchini and eggplant to give a striped effect.

2 Cut the zucchini, eggplant and carrot into strips about 4 inches long and ⅛ inch wide.

3 Put the zucchini, eggplant and carrot in a colander and sprinkle liberally with salt. Leave for about 30 minutes, then rinse thoroughly under cold running water. Drain well.

4 Thinly slice the onion from top to base, discarding the plump pieces in the middle. Separate the layers so that there are lots of fine, long strips. Mix all the vegetables together and season with salt and pepper.

5 Make the batter just before frying. Combine the egg and ice water in a bowl, then sift in the flour. Mix briefly with a fork or chopsticks. Do not overmix; the batter should remain lumpy. Add the vegetables to the batter and mix to combine.

6 Half-fill a wok with oil and heat to 350°F. Scoop up one heaped tablespoon of the mixture at a time and carefully lower it into the oil. Deep-fry in batches for about 3 minutes, or until golden brown and crisp. Drain on paper towels. Serve each portion with sea salt flakes, slices of lemon and a tiny bowl of Japanese soy sauce for dipping.

Spicy Spareribs

Fragrant with spices, this authentic Chinese dish makes a great—if slightly messy—appetizer to an informal meal.

INGREDIENTS

Serves 4
1½–2 pounds meaty pork spareribs
1 teaspoon Szechuan peppercorns
2 tablespoons sea salt
½ teaspoon Chinese five-spice powder
1½ tablespoons cornstarch
peanut oil, for deep-frying
cilantro sprigs, to garnish

For the marinade
2 tablespoons light soy sauce
1 teaspoon superfine sugar
1 tablespoon Chinese rice wine or
   dry sherry
freshly ground black pepper

1 Using a sharp, heavy cleaver, chop the spareribs into pieces about 2 inches long, or ask your butcher to do this for you. Place them in a shallow dish and set aside.

2 Heat a wok to medium heat. Add the Szechuan peppercorns and salt and dry-fry for about 3 minutes, stirring constantly, until the mixture colors slightly. Remove from the heat and stir in the five-spice powder. Set aside to cool.

3 Grind the cooled spice mixture to a fine powder in a mortar with a pestle.

4 Sprinkle 1 teaspoon of the spice powder over the spareribs and rub in well with your hands. To make the marinade, add all the ingredients and toss the ribs to coat thoroughly. Cover and marinate in the refrigerator for about 2 hours, turning occasionally.

5 Pour off any excess marinade from the spareribs. Sprinkle the ribs with the cornstarch and mix to coat evenly.

6 Half-fill a wok with oil and heat to 350°F. Deep-fry the spareribs in batches for 3 minutes, or until golden. Remove and set aside. When all the batches have been cooked, reheat the oil to 350°F and deep-fry the ribs for a second time for 1–2 minutes, or until crisp and thoroughly cooked. Drain on paper towels. Transfer the ribs to a warm serving platter and sprinkle with 1–1½ teaspoons of the remaining spice powder. Garnish with cilantro sprigs and serve immediately.

Barbecue-glazed Chicken Skewers

Known as *yakitori*, this appetizer is often served with predinner drinks in Japan.

INGREDIENTS

Makes 12 skewers and 8 wing pieces
4 chicken thighs, skinned
4 scallions, blanched and cut into short lengths
8 chicken wings
1 tablespoon grated daikon, to serve (optional)

For the sauce
4 tablespoons sake
5 tablespoons dark soy sauce
2 tablespoons tamari sauce
3 tablespoons sweet sherry
¼ cup sugar

1 Bone the chicken thighs and cut the meat into large dice. Thread the scallions and chicken onto 12 bamboo skewers.

2 To prepare the chicken wings, remove the tip at the first joint. Chop through the second joint, revealing the two narrow bones. Take hold of the bones with a clean cloth and pull, turning the meat around the bones inside out. Remove the smaller bone and set the meat aside.

3 To make the sauce, combine all the sauce ingredients in a stainless steel or enamel saucepan and simmer until reduced by two-thirds. Set aside to cool.

4 Cook the skewers of chicken and the wings under a preheated broiler without brushing on any oil. When juices begin to emerge from the chicken, baste liberally with the sauce. Cook the chicken on the skewers for another 3 minutes and cook the wings for another 5 minutes. Serve with grated daikon, if desired.

Lacy Duck Egg Nets

You can find duck eggs in good Asian supermarkets or order them direct from farms, but regular eggs are also good here. Thais have a special dispenser to make the net, but you can use a pastry bag fitted with a small nozzle or a squeeze bottle.

INGREDIENTS

Makes about 12–15
For the filling
4 cilantro roots
2 garlic cloves
10 white peppercorns
pinch of salt
3 tablespoons oil
1 small onion, finely chopped
4 ounces lean ground pork
3 ounces shelled shrimp, chopped
$\frac{1}{2}$ cup roasted peanuts, ground
1 teaspoon palm sugar
fish sauce, to taste

For the egg nets
6 duck eggs or jumbo hen eggs
cilantro leaves, to serve, plus extra
  to garnish
scallion tassels and sliced red chillies,
  to garnish

1 Using a mortar and pestle, grind the cilantro roots, garlic, white peppercorns and salt into a paste.

2 Heat 2 tablespoons of the oil, add the paste and fry until fragrant. Add the onion and cook until softened. Add the pork and shrimp and continue to stir-fry until the meat is cooked.

3 Add the peanuts, palm sugar, salt and fish sauce, to taste. Stir the mixture and continue to cook until it becomes a little sticky. Remove from the heat. Transfer the mixture to a bowl and set aside.

4 Break the eggs into a bowl, and beat with a fork. Grease a non-stick frying pan with the remaining oil and heat. Using a special dispenser or a suitable alternative, trail the eggs across the pan to make a net pattern, about 5 inches in diameter.

5 When the net is set, carefully remove it from the pan, and repeat until all the eggs have been used up.

6 To assemble, lay a net on a board, lay a few cilantro leaves on it and top with a spoonful of filling. Turn in the edges to make a neat square shape. Repeat with the rest of the nets. Arrange on a serving dish and garnish with the fresh cilantro leaves, scallion tassels and chilies.

Pickled Sweet-and-Sour Cucumber

The "pickling" can be done in minutes rather than days—but the more time you have, the better the result.

INGREDIENTS

Serves 6–8
1 slender cucumber, about
   12 inches long
1 teaspoon salt
2 teaspoons superfine sugar
1 teaspoon rice vinegar
½ teaspoon red chili oil (optional)
few drops of sesame oil

1 Halve the unpeeled cucumber lengthwise. Scrape out the seeds and cut the cucumber into thick chunks.

2 In a bowl, sprinkle the cucumber chunks with the salt and mix well. Leave for at least 20–30 minutes—longer if possible—then pour the liquid off.

3 Mix the cucumber with the sugar, vinegar and chili oil, if using. Sprinkle with the sesame oil just before serving.

Hot-and-Sour Cabbage

This popular dish from Szechuan in western China can be served hot or cold.

INGREDIENTS

Serves 6–8
1 pound pale green or white cabbage
3–4 tablespoons vegetable oil
10–12 red Szechuan peppercorns
few whole dried red chilies
1 teaspoon salt
1 tablespoon light brown sugar
1 tablespoon light soy sauce
2 tablespoons rice vinegar
few drops of sesame oil

1 Cut the cabbage leaves into small pieces, each roughly 1 x ½ inch.

2 Heat the oil in a preheated wok until smoking, then add the peppercorns and chilies.

3 Add the cabbage to the wok and stir-fry for about 2 minutes. Add the salt and sugar, continue stirring for 1 minute more, then add the soy sauce, vinegar and sesame oil. Blend well and serve immediately.

Spicy Meat Patties with Coconut

Spicy meat patties, known as *Rempah*, with a hint of coconut, often feature as one of the delicious accompaniments in an Indonesian-style buffet.

INGREDIENTS

Makes 22

4 ounces freshly grated coconut, or
   dried coconut, soaked in
   4–6 tablespoons boiling water
12 ounces finely ground beef
½ teaspoon each coriander and cumin
   seeds, dry-fried
1 garlic clove, crushed
a little beaten egg
1–2 tablespoons flour
peanut oil for frying
salt
thin lemon or lime wedges, to serve

1 Mix the moistened coconut with the ground beef.

2 Grind the dry-fried coriander and cumin seeds with a mortar and pestle. Add the ground spices to the meat and coconut mixture together with the garlic, salt to taste, and sufficient beaten egg to bind.

3 Divide the meat into even-size portions, the size of a walnut, and form into patty shapes.

4 Dust with flour. Heat the oil and shallow fry the patties for 4–5 minutes until both sides are golden brown and cooked through. Serve with lemon or lime wedges, to squeeze over.

Corn Fritters

There is no doubt that freshly cooked corn is best for this recipe, called *Perkedel Jagung*. Do not add salt to the water, because this toughens the outer husk.

INGREDIENTS

Makes 20

2 fresh corn on the cob, or 12-ounce
   can corn kernels
2 macadamia nuts or 4 almonds
1 garlic clove
1 onion, quartered
½ inch fresh *laos*, peeled
   and sliced
1 teaspoon ground coriander
2–3 tablespoons oil
3 eggs, beaten
2 tablespoons dried coconut
2 scallions, finely shredded
a few celery leaves, finely
   shredded (optional)
salt

1 Cook the corn on the cob in boiling water for 7–8 minutes. Drain, cool slightly and, using a sharp knife, strip the kernels from the cob. If using canned corn kernels, drain well.

2 Grind the nuts, garlic, onion, *laos* and coriander to a fine paste in a food processor or mortar and pestle. Heat a little oil and fry the paste until it gives off a spicy aroma.

3 Add the fried spices to the beaten eggs with the coconut, scallions and celery leaves, if using. Add salt to taste with the corn kernels.

4 Heat the remaining oil in a shallow frying pan. Drop large spoonfuls of batter into the pan and cook for about 2–3 minutes until golden. Flip the fritters over with a metal spatula and cook until golden brown and crispy. Cook three or four fritters at a time.

FISH AND SEAFOOD

The many islands in the Pacific and the long coastline of mainland China ensure an abundance of wonderful fish and seafood recipes in the cuisines of Asia. Whole fish and fillets are combined with fragrant herbs and marinades and then steamed, baked or fried quickly. The different ways of preparing shrimp, mussels, scallops, squid and other seafood are almost endless, from the subtly aromatic Pan-steamed Mussels with Thai Herbs to the robust and spicy Shrimp with Chayote in Turmeric Sauce. All are quick to prepare, highly nutritious and utterly delicious.

Steamed Fish with Ginger and Scallions

Firm and delicate fish steaks, such as salmon or turbot, can be cooked by this same method.

INGREDIENTS

Serves 4–6

1 sea bass, sea trout or red snapper, weighing about 1½ pounds, cleaned
½ teaspoon salt
1 tablespoon sesame oil
2–3 scallions, cut in half lengthwise
2 tablespoons light soy sauce
2 tablespoons Chinese rice wine or dry sherry
1 tablespoon fresh ginger, cut into fine strips
2 tablespoons vegetable oil
scallions, cut into fine strips, to garnish

1 Using a sharp knife, score both sides of the fish as far down as the bone with diagonal cuts about 1 inch apart. Rub the fish all over, inside and out, with salt and sesame oil.

2 Sprinkle the scallions over a heatproof platter and place the fish on top. Blend together the soy sauce and rice wine or dry sherry with the ginger and pour evenly all over the fish.

3 Place the platter in a very hot steamer (or inside a wok on a rack) and steam vigorously, covered, for 12–15 minutes.

4 Heat the vegetable oil until hot. Remove the platter from the steamer, place the scallions on top of the fish, then pour the hot oil along the whole length of the fish. Serve immediately.

Fried Monkfish Coated with Rice Noodles

These marinated medallions of fish are coated in rice vermicelli and deep-fried – they taste as good as they look.

INGREDIENTS

Serves 4

1 pound monkfish
1 teaspoon grated fresh ginger
1 garlic clove, finely chopped
2 tablespoons soy sauce
6 ounces rice vermicelli
4 tablespoons cornstarch
2 eggs, beaten
salt and freshly ground black pepper
oil for deep-frying
banana leaves, to serve (optional)

For the dipping sauce

2 tablespoons soy sauce
2 tablespoons rice vinegar
1 tablespoon sugar
2 red chilies, thinly sliced
1 scallion, thinly sliced

1 Trim the monkfish, and cut into 1-inch thick medallions. Place in a dish, and add the ginger, garlic and soy sauce. Mix lightly, and let marinate for 10 minutes.

2 Meanwhile, make the dipping sauce. Combine the soy sauce, vinegar and sugar in a small saucepan. Bring to a boil. Add salt and pepper to taste. Remove from the heat, add the chilies and scallion, and then set aside until required.

3 Using kitchen scissors, cut the noodles into 1½-inch lengths. Spread them out in a shallow bowl.

4 Lightly coat the fish medallions in cornstarch, dip in beaten egg, and cover with noodles, pressing them on to the fish so that they stick.

5 Deep-fry the coated fish in hot oil, two to three pieces at a time, until the noodle coating is fluffy, crisp and light golden brown. Drain, and serve hot on banana leaves, if you like, accompanied by the dipping sauce.

Fish with Sweet-and-Sour Sauce

Another name for this dish is
Five-Willow Fish, after the five
vegetables in the sweet-and-sour
sauce.

INGREDIENTS

Serves 4–6

1 carp, red snapper, sea bass, trout,
grouper or pompano, weighing about
1½ pounds, cleaned
1 teaspoon salt
about 2 tablespoons all-purpose flour
vegetable oil, for deep-frying
fresh cilantro leaves, to garnish

For the sauce

1 tablespoon vegetable oil
1 medium carrot, cut into fine strips
2 ounces bamboo shoots, cut into strips
1 ounce green bell pepper, seeded and
cut into fine strips
1 ounce red bell pepper, seeded and cut
into fine strips
2–3 scallions, cut into fine strips
1 tablespoon finely chopped fresh
ginger
1 tablespoon light soy sauce
2 tablespoons light brown sugar
2–3 tablespoons rice vinegar
about ½ cup Basic Broth
1 tablespoon cornstarch paste

1 Clean and dry the fish well. Using
a sharp knife, score both sides of
the fish as deep as the bone with
diagonal cuts at intervals of about 1 inch.

2 Rub the whole fish with salt both
inside and out, then coat it from
head to tail with flour.

3 Heat the oil in a wok or frying pan
and deep-fry the fish for about 3–4
minutes on both sides, or until golden
brown. Remove the fish and drain,
then place on a warmed serving platter.

4 For the sauce, heat the oil in a
preheated clean pan or wok and
stir-fry all the vegetables for about
1 minute, then add the ginger, soy
sauce, sugar and vinegar. Blend well,
add the broth and bring to a boil. Add
the cornstarch paste, stirring until thick
and smooth. Pour over the fish and
serve, garnished with cilantro leaves.

Sesame Baked Fish with a Hot Ginger Marinade

Although tropical varieties of fish are found increasingly frequently in supermarkets, Oriental food stores usually have a wider selection suitable for this Malaysian dish.

INGREDIENTS
Serves 4–6
2 red snapper, or monkfish, heads off, each weighing 12 ounces
2 tablespoons vegetable oil, plus extra for greasing
2 teaspoons sesame oil
2 tablespoons sesame seeds
1-inch piece fresh ginger, thinly sliced
2 garlic cloves, crushed
2 small fresh red chilies, seeded and finely chopped
4 shallots or 1 medium onion, halved and sliced
2 tablespoons water
½-inch square shrimp paste or 1 tablespoon fish sauce
2 teaspoons sugar
½ teaspoon cracked black pepper
juice of 2 limes
3–4 banana leaves (optional)

1 Clean and dry the fish well. Slash both sides of the fish deeply with a sharp knife.

2 To make the marinade, heat the vegetable and sesame oils in a preheated wok. Add the sesame seeds and fry until golden. Add the ginger, garlic, chilies and shallots or onion and stir-fry 1–2 minutes, or until softened. Add the water, shrimp paste or fish sauce, sugar, pepper and lime juice and simmer for 2–3 minutes. Remove from the heat and allow to cool.

COOK'S TIP

Banana leaves are available from Indian and Southeast Asian food stores.

3 If using banana leaves, remove and discard the central stems. Soften the leaves by dipping them in boiling water. To keep them supple, rub the surfaces with vegetable oil. Spread the sesame seed marinade over the fish, then wrap them separately in the banana leaves, secured with a skewer, or enclose them in foil. Set aside in a cool place to allow the flavors to mingle, for up to 3 hours.

4 Place the wrapped fish on a baking sheet and cook in a preheated oven at 350°F or on a glowing barbecue for 35–40 minutes. Serve hot.

Sizzling Chinese Steamed Fish

Steamed whole fish is very popular in China, where the wok is used as a steamer. In this recipe the fish is flavored with garlic, ginger and scallions cooked in sizzling hot oil.

INGREDIENTS

Serves 4

4 rainbow trout, about 9 ounces each
¼ teaspoon salt
½ teaspoon sugar
2 garlic cloves, finely chopped
1 tablespoon finely diced fresh ginger
5 scallions, cut into 2-inch lengths and then into fine strips
¼ cup peanut oil
1 teaspoon sesame oil
3 tablespoons light soy sauce
thread egg noodles and stir-fried vegetables, to serve

1 Make three diagonal slits on both sides of each fish and lay them on a heatproof plate. Place a small rack or trivet in a wok half-filled with water, cover and heat until just simmering.

2 Sprinkle the fish with the salt, sugar, garlic and ginger. Place the plate securely on the rack or trivet and cover. Steam gently for about 12 minutes, or until the flesh has turned pale pink and feels quite firm.

3 Turn off the heat, remove the lid and scatter the scallions over the fish. Replace the lid.

4 Heat the peanut and sesame oils in a small pan over high heat until just smoking, then quickly pour a quarter over the scallions on each of the fish—the scallions will sizzle and cook in the hot oil. Sprinkle the soy sauce over the top. Serve the fish and juices immediately with boiled noodles and stir-fried vegetables.

Chinese-spiced Fish Fillets

INGREDIENTS

Serves 4

generous ½ cup all-purpose flour
1 teaspoon Chinese five-spice powder
8 skinless fillets of fish, such as flounder
   or lemon sole, about 2 pounds total
1 egg, lightly beaten
scant 1 cup fine fresh bread crumbs
peanut oil, for frying
2 tablespoons butter
4 scallions, cut diagonally into thin
   slices
12 ounces tomatoes, seeded and diced
2 tablespoons soy sauce
salt and freshly ground black pepper
red bell pepper strips and chives,
   to garnish

1 Sift the flour together with the Chinese five-spice powder and salt and pepper to taste onto a plate. Dip the fish fillets first in the seasoned flour, then in the beaten egg and finally in bread crumbs.

2 Pour oil into a large frying pan to a depth of ½ inch. Heat until it is very hot and starting to sizzle. Add the coated fillets, a few at a time, and fry for 2–3 minutes on each side, depending on their thickness, until just cooked and golden brown. Do not crowd the pan, or the temperature of the oil will drop and the fish will absorb too much of it.

3 Drain the fillets on paper towels, then transfer to serving plates and keep warm. Pour off all the oil from the frying pan and wipe it out with paper towels.

4 Cook the scallions and tomatoes in the butter for 1 minute, then add the soy sauce.

5 Spoon the tomato mixture over the fish, garnish with red bell pepper strips and chives and serve.

Fish with a Cashew-Ginger Marinade

To capture the sweet, spicy flavor of this Indonesian favorite, marinated fish are wrapped in foil before baking. When they are unwrapped at the table, their delicious aroma will make your mouth water.

INGREDIENTS

Serves 4

2½ pounds sea bass or halibut, scaled and cleaned
1¼ cups raw cashews
2 shallots or 1 small onion, finely chopped
½-inch piece fresh ginger, finely chopped
1 garlic clove, crushed
1 small fresh red chili, seeded and finely chopped
2 tablespoons vegetable oil
1 tablespoon shrimp paste
2 teaspoons sugar
2 tablespoons tamarind sauce
2 tablespoons ketchup
juice of 2 limes
salt

3 Cover both sides of each fish with the paste and set aside in the refrigerator for up to 8 hours to allow the flavors to mingle.

4 Wrap the fish in foil, securing the parcels carefully. Bake in a preheated oven at 350°F for 30–35 minutes.

1 Slash the fish 3 or 4 times on each side with a sharp knife. Set aside.

2 Grind the cashews, shallots or onion, ginger, garlic and chili to a fine paste in a mortar with a pestle or in a food processor. Add the vegetable oil, shrimp paste and sugar and season to taste with salt. Blend, then add the tamarind sauce, ketchup and lime juice and blend again.

Whole Fish with Sweet-and-sour Sauce

INGREDIENTS

Serves 4

1 whole fish, such as red snapper or
  carp, about 2¼ pounds prepared
2–3 tablespoons cornstarch
oil for frying
salt and freshly ground black pepper
boiled rice, to serve

For the spice paste
2 garlic cloves
2 lemon grass stems
1 inch fresh *laos*
1 inch fresh ginger root
¾ inch fresh turmeric or
  ½ teaspoon ground turmeric
5 macadamia nuts or 10 almonds

For the sauce
1 tablespoon brown sugar
3 tablespoons cider vinegar
about 1½ cups water
2 lime leaves, torn
4 shallots, quartered
3 tomatoes, skinned and cut in wedges
3 scallions, finely shredded
1 fresh red chili, seeded and shredded

1 Wash and dry the fish thoroughly
and then sprinkle it inside and out
with salt. Set aside for 15 minutes,
while preparing the other ingredients.

2 Peel and crush the garlic cloves.
Use only the lower white part of
the lemon grass stems and slice thinly.
Peel and slice the fresh *laos*, the ginger
root and turmeric, if using. Grind the
nuts, garlic, lemon grass, *laos*, ginger
and turmeric to a fine paste in
a food processor or with a mortar
and pestle.

3 Scrape the paste into a bowl. Stir
in the brown sugar, cider vinegar,
seasoning to taste and the water. Add
the lime leaves.

4 Dust the fish with the cornstarch
and fry on both sides in hot oil for
about 8–9 minutes or until almost
cooked through. Drain the fish on
paper towels and transfer to a serving
dish. Keep warm.

5 Pour off most of the oil and then
pour in the spicy liquid and allow
to come to a boil. Reduce the heat and
cook for 3–4 minutes. Add the shallots
and tomatoes, followed a minute later
by the scallions and chili. Taste and
adjust the seasoning.

6 Pour the sauce over the fish. Serve
at once, with plenty of rice.

Sea Bass with Chinese Chives

Chinese chives are widely
available in Asian supermarkets
but if you are unable to buy
them, use half a large Spanish
onion, finely sliced, instead.

INGREDIENTS

Serves 4
2 sea bass, about 1 pound total
1 tablespoon cornstarch
3 tablespoons vegetable oil
6 ounces Chinese chives
1 tablespoon Chinese rice wine or
    dry sherry
1 teaspoon superfine sugar
salt and freshly ground black pepper
Chinese chives with flower heads,
    to garnish

1 Remove the scales from the bass by
scraping them with the back of a
knife, working from the tail end toward
the head end. Fillet the fish. Your
fishmonger could do this for you.

2 Cut the fillets into large chunks
and dust them lightly with
cornstarch, salt and pepper.

3 Heat 2 tablespoons of the oil in a
preheated wok. When the oil is
hot, toss the chunks of fish in the wok
briefly to seal, then set aside. Wipe out
the wok with paper towels.

4 Cut the Chinese chives into 2-inch
lengths and discard the flowers.
Reheat the wok and add the remaining
oil, then stir-fry the Chinese chives for
30 seconds. Add the fish and rice wine
or dry sherry, then bring to a boil and
stir in the sugar. Serve hot, garnished
with some flowering Chinese chives.

Salt-grilled Mackerel

In Japan salt is applied to oily fish before cooking to draw out the flavors. Mackerel and snapper are the most popular choices for this treatment, known as *Shio-yaki* in Japanese. The fish develop a unique flavor and texture when treated with salt. The salt is washed away before cooking.

INGREDIENTS

Serves 2
2 small or 1 large mackerel or snapper, gutted and cleaned, with head on
1 tablespoon salt
1 medium carrot, shredded, to serve

For the soy-ginger dip
¼ cup dark soy sauce
2 tablespoons sugar
1-inch piece fresh ginger

For the Japanese horseradish
3 tablespoons wasabi powder
2 teaspoons water

1 To make the soy-ginger dip, put the soy sauce, sugar and ginger in a stainless steel saucepan. Bring to a boil, lower the heat and simmer for 2–3 minutes. Strain and set aside to cool. To make the Japanese horseradish, put the wasabi powder in a small bowl and stir in the water to make a stiff paste. Shape the mixture into a neat ball and set aside.

> COOK'S TIP
>
> Wasabi is the ground root of an Asian type of horseradish. It is very sharp and aromatic and often served with raw fish and shellfish. In the West, it is usually available only as a powder, which has to be mixed with water to make a paste.

2 Rinse the fish under cold, running water and pat thoroughly dry with paper towels. Slash the fish several times on both sides, cutting down as far as the bone. Sprinkle the salt inside the fish and rub it well into the skin. Set aside on a plate for 40 minutes.

3 Wash the fish in plenty of cold water to remove all traces of salt. Shape the fish neatly and secure in position with two bamboo skewers inserted along the length of the body, one above and one below the eye.

4 Cook the fish under a preheated broiler or on a grill for 10 to 12 minutes, or until it is cooked, turning once. The skin can be basted with a little of the soy-ginger dip partway through cooking, if desired. Transfer the fish to a serving plate and arrange carrot, Japanese horseradish and soy-ginger dip decoratively around it.

Gingered Seafood Stir-fry

This cornucopia of scallops, shrimp and squid in an aromatic sauce makes a refreshing summer supper, served with plenty of crusty bread to mop up the juices—together with a glass of chilled dry white wine. It would also make a great dinner-party appetizer for four people.

INGREDIENTS

Serves 2

1 tablespoon sunflower oil
1 teaspoon sesame oil
1-inch piece fresh ginger, finely
  chopped
1 bunch scallions, sliced
1 red bell pepper, seeded and finely
  chopped
4 ounces bay scallops
8 jumbo shrimp, peeled
4 ounces squid rings
1 tablespoon lime juice
1 tablespoon light soy sauce
4 tablespoons coconut milk
salt and freshly ground black pepper
mixed salad greens and lime slices,
  to serve

1 Heat the sunflower and sesame oils in a preheated wok or large frying pan and cook the ginger and scallions for 2–3 minutes, or until golden. Stir in the red bell pepper and cook for another 3 minutes.

2 Add the scallops, shrimp and squid rings and cook over medium heat for about 3 minutes, or until the seafood is just cooked.

3 Stir in the lime juice, soy sauce and coconut milk. Simmer, uncovered, for 2 minutes, or until the juices begin to thicken slightly.

4 Season well. Arrange the salad greens on two serving plates and spoon the seafood mixture with the juices on top. Serve with lime slices for squeezing over the seafood.

Spiced Scallops in their Shells

Scallops are excellent steamed. When served with this spicy sauce, they make a delicious, yet simple, appetizer for four people or a light lunch for two. Each person spoons sauce onto the scallops before eating them.

INGREDIENTS

Serves 2
8 scallops, shelled (ask the fishmonger to reserve the cupped side of 4 shells)
2 slices fresh ginger, shredded
½ garlic clove, shredded
2 scallions, green parts only, cut into fine strips
salt and freshly ground black pepper

For the sauce
1 garlic clove, crushed
1 tablespoon grated fresh ginger
2 scallions, white parts only, chopped
1–2 fresh green chilies, seeded and finely chopped
1 tablespoon light soy sauce
1 tablespoon dark soy sauce
2 teaspoons sesame oil

1 Remove the dark beardlike fringe and tough muscle from the scallops.

2 Place 2 scallops in each shell. Season lightly with salt and pepper, then scatter the ginger, garlic and scallions on top. Place the shells in a bamboo steamer in a wok and steam for about 6 minutes, or until the scallops look opaque (you may have to do this in batches).

3 Meanwhile, make the sauce. Mix together the garlic, ginger, scallions, chilies, soy sauces and sesame oil and pour into a small serving bowl.

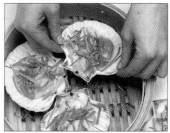

4 Carefully remove each shell from the steamer, taking care not to spill the juices, and arrange them on a serving plate with the sauce bowl in the center. Serve at once.

Chili Shrimp

This delightful, spicy combination makes a lovely, light main course for a casual supper. Serve with rice, noodles or even freshly cooked pasta and a leafy green salad.

INGREDIENTS

Serves 3–4
3 tablespoons olive oil
2 shallots, chopped
2 garlic cloves, chopped
1 fresh red chili, chopped
1 pound ripe tomatoes, skinned, seeded and chopped
1 tablespoon tomato paste
1 bay leaf
1 thyme sprig
6 tablespoons dry white wine
1 pound cooked jumbo shrimp, peeled
salt and freshly ground black pepper
roughly torn basil leaves, to garnish

1 Heat the oil in a pan, then add the shallots, garlic and chili and stir-fry until the garlic starts to brown.

2 Add the tomatoes, tomato paste, bay leaf, thyme, wine and seasoning. Bring to a boil, then reduce the heat and cook gently for about 10 minutes, stirring occasionally, until the sauce has thickened. Discard the herbs.

3 Stir the shrimp into the sauce and heat through for a few minutes. Taste and adjust the seasoning. Scatter the basil leaves on top and serve at once.

> ——— COOK'S TIP ———
>
> For a milder flavor, remove all the seeds from the chili.

Scallops with Ginger

Scallops are of course at their best fresh, but are available frozen throughout the year. Rich and creamy, this dish is very simple to make and utterly scrumptious.

INGREDIENTS

Serves 4
8–12 scallops
3 tablespoons butter
1-inch piece fresh ginger, finely chopped
1 bunch scallions, sliced diagonally
4 tablespoons white vermouth
1 cup crème fraîche or half-and-half
salt and freshly ground black pepper
chopped fresh parsley, to garnish

1 Remove the tough muscle opposite the coral on each scallop. Separate the coral and cut the white part of the scallop in half horizontally.

2 Melt the butter in a frying pan. Add the scallops, including the corals, and sauté for about 2 minutes, or until lightly browned. Take care not to overcook the scallops, as this will make them tough.

3 Lift out the scallops with a slotted spoon and transfer to a warmed serving dish. Keep warm.

4 Add the ginger and scallions to the pan and stir-fry for 2 minutes. Pour in the vermouth and allow to bubble until it has almost evaporated. Stir in the crème fraîche or half-and-half and cook for a few minutes, until the sauce has thickened. Season to taste.

5 Pour the sauce over the scallops, sprinkle with parsley and serve immediately.

Salmon Teriyaki

Marinating the salmon makes it so wonderfully tender it just melts in the mouth; the crunchy condiment provides an excellent foil.

INGREDIENTS

Serves 4
1½ pounds salmon fillet
2 tablespoons sunflower oil
watercress, to garnish

For the teriyaki sauce

1 teaspoon superfine sugar
1 teaspoon dry white wine
1 teaspoon sake, rice wine or
    dry sherry
2 tablespoons dark soy sauce

For the condiment

2 inch piece fresh ginger, thinly sliced
pink food coloring (optional)
2 ounces daikon, grated

1 For the teriyaki sauce, combine the sugar, white wine, sake or rice wine or dry sherry and soy sauce, stirring until the sugar dissolves.

2 Remove the skin from the salmon using a very sharp filleting knife.

3 Cut the fillet into strips, then place in a nonmetallic dish. Pour the teriyaki sauce over the fish and set aside to marinate for 10–15 minutes.

4 To make the condiment, place the ginger in a bowl and add a little pink food coloring if you wish. Stir in the daikon.

5 Lift the salmon from the teriyaki sauce and drain.

6 Heat the oil in a preheated wok. Add the salmon in batches and stir-fry for 3–4 minutes, or until it is cooked. Transfer to serving plates, garnish with the watercress and serve with the daikon and ginger condiment.

Lemongrass-and-Basil-scented Mussels

The classic Thai flavorings of lemongrass and basil are used in this fragrant dish.

INGREDIENTS

Serves 4

4–4½ pounds fresh mussels in
    their shells
2 lemongrass stalks
5–6 fresh basil sprigs
2-inch piece fresh ginger, finely chopped
2 shallots, finely chopped
⅔ cup fish broth

1 Scrub the mussels under cold running water, scraping off any barnacles with a small, sharp knife. Pull or cut off the hairy "beards." Discard any mussels with damaged shells and any that remain open when they are sharply tapped.

2 Cut each lemongrass stalk in half and bruise with a rolling pin.

3 Pull the basil leaves off the stems and roughly chop half of them. Reserve the remainder.

4 Put the mussels, lemongrass, chopped basil, shallots, ginger and broth in a wok. Bring to a boil, cover and simmer for 5 minutes. Discard the lemongrass and any mussels that remain closed, scatter the reserved basil leaves on top, and serve immediately.

Baked Crab with Scallions and Ginger

This recipe is far less complicated than it looks and will delight the eye as much as the taste buds.

INGREDIENTS

Serves 4

1 large or 2 medium crabs, about
  1½ pounds total
2 tablespoons Chinese rice wine or
  dry sherry
1 egg, lightly beaten
1 tablespoon cornstarch
3–4 tablespoons vegetable oil
1 tablespoon finely chopped
  fresh ginger
3–4 scallions, cut into short lengths
2 tablespoons soy sauce
1 teaspoon light brown sugar
about 5 tablespoons Basic Broth
few drops of sesame oil

1 Cut the crab in half from the underbelly. Break off the claws and crack them with the back of a cleaver. Discard the legs and crack the shell, breaking it into several pieces. Discard the feathery gills and the sac. Put the pieces of crab in a bowl.

2 Combine the rice wine or dry sherry, egg and cornstarch and pour over the crab. Marinate for 10–15 minutes.

3 Heat the oil in a preheated wok. Add the crab pieces, ginger and scallions and stir-fry for 2 to 3 minutes.

4 Add the soy sauce, sugar and broth and blend well. Bring to a boil, reduce the heat, cover and braise for 3–4 minutes, or until it is cooked. Transfer the crab to a serving dish, sprinkle with the sesame oil and serve.

--- COOK'S TIP ---

For the very best flavor, buy a live crab and cook it yourself. However, if you prefer to buy a cooked crab, look for one that feels heavy for its size. This is an indication that it has fully grown into its shell and that there will be plenty of meat. Male crabs have larger claws and so will yield a greater proportion of white meat. However, females—identifiable by a broader, less pointed tail flap—may contain coral, which many people regard as a delicacy.

Pan-steamed Mussels with Thai Herbs

Another simple dish to prepare. The lemongrass adds a refreshing tang to the mussels.

INGREDIENTS

Serves 4–6

2¼ pounds mussels, cleaned and
   beards removed
2 lemongrass stalks, finely chopped
4 shallots, chopped
4 kaffir lime leaves, coarsely torn
2 red chilies, sliced
1 tablespoon fish sauce
2 tablespoons lime juice
2 scallions, chopped, to garnish
cilantro leaves, to garnish

1 Place all the ingredients, except for the scallions and cilantro, in a large saucepan and stir thoroughly.

2 Cover and steam for 5–7 minutes, shaking the saucepan occasionally, until the mussels open. Discard any mussels that remain closed.

3 Transfer the cooked mussels to a serving platter.

4 Garnish the mussels with chopped scallions and cilantro leaves. Serve the dish immediately.

Pineapple Curry with Shrimp and Mussels

The delicate sweet-and-sour flavor of this curry comes from the pineapple and, although it seems an odd combination, it is rather delicious. Use the freshest shellfish that you can find.

INGREDIENTS

Serves 4–6

2½ cups unsweetened coconut milk
2 tablespoons red curry paste
2 tablespoons fish sauce
1 tablespoon sugar
8 ounces jumbo shrimp, shelled
    and deveined
1 pound mussels, cleaned and
    beards removed
6 ounces fresh pineapple, finely crushed
    or chopped
5 kaffir lime leaves, torn
2 red chilies, chopped, and cilantro
    leaves, to garnish

1 In a large saucepan, bring half the coconut milk to a boil and heat, stirring, until it separates.

2 Add the red curry paste and cook until fragrant. Add the fish sauce and sugar and continue to cook for a few moments.

3 Stir in the rest of the coconut milk and bring back to a boil. Add the jumbo shrimp, mussels, pineapple and kaffir lime leaves.

4 Reheat until boiling and then simmer for 3–5 minutes, until the shrimp are cooked and the mussels have opened. Remove any mussels that have not opened and discard. Serve garnished with chopped red chilies and cilantro leaves.

Curried Shrimp in Coconut Milk

A curry-like dish where the shrimp are cooked in a spicy coconut gravy.

INGREDIENTS

Serves 4–6

2½ cups unsweetened coconut milk
2 tablespoons yellow curry paste
    (see Cook's Tip)
1 tablespoon fish sauce
½ teaspoon salt
1 teaspoon sugar
1 pound jumbo shrimp, shelled, tails
    left intact and deveined
8 ounces cherry tomatoes
juice of ½ lime, to serve
2 red chilies, cut into strips, and
    cilantro leaves, to garnish

1 Put half the coconut milk into a pan or wok and bring to a boil.

2 Add the yellow curry paste to the coconut milk, stir until it disperses, then simmer for about 10 minutes.

3 Add the fish sauce, salt, sugar and remaining coconut milk. Simmer for another 5 minutes.

4 Add the shrimp and cherry tomatoes. Simmer very gently for about 5 minutes until the shrimp are pink and tender.

5 Serve sprinkled with lime juice and garnished with chilies and cilantro.

COOK'S TIP

To make yellow curry paste, process 6–8 yellow chilies, 1 chopped lemongrass stalk, 4 peeled shallots, 4 garlic cloves, 1 tablespoon peeled chopped fresh ginger, 1 teaspoon coriander seeds, 1 teaspoon mustard powder, 1 teaspoon salt, ½ teaspoon ground cinnamon, 1 tablespoon light brown sugar and 2 tablespoons oil in a blender or food processor. When a paste forms, transfer to a jar and keep in the fridge.

Baked Lobster with Black Beans

The term "baked," as used on
most Chinese restaurant menus,
is not strictly correct—
"pot-roasted" or "pan-baked" is
more accurate.

INGREDIENTS

Serves 4–6

1 large or 2 medium lobsters, about
   1¼ pounds total
vegetable oil, for deep-frying
1 garlic clove, finely chopped
1 teaspoon finely chopped fresh
   ginger
2–3 scallions, chopped
2 tablespoons black bean sauce
2 tablespoons Chinese rice wine or
   dry sherry
½ cup Basic Broth
fresh cilantro leaves, to garnish

1 Starting from the head, cut the
lobster in half lengthwise. Discard
the legs, remove the claws and crack
them with the back of a cleaver.
Discard the feathery lungs and
intestine. Cut each half into 4–5 pieces.

2 Heat the oil in a preheated wok
and deep-fry the lobster pieces for
about 2 minutes, or until the shells turn
bright orange. Remove the pieces from
the wok and drain on paper towels.

3 Pour off the excess oil, leaving
about 1 tablespoon in the wok.
Add the garlic, ginger, scallions and
black bean sauce and stir-fry for
1 minute.

4 Add the lobster pieces to the sauce
and blend well. Add the rice wine
or dry sherry and broth, bring to a boil,
cover and cook for 2–3 minutes. Serve
garnished with cilantro leaves.

COOK'S TIP

Ideally, buy live lobsters and cook them
yourself. Ready-cooked ones have usually
been boiled for far too long and have lost
much of their delicate flavor and texture.

Shrimp Curry with Quail Eggs

This luscious Indonesian recipe is characterized by the mix of flavors—galangal, chilies, turmeric and coconut milk.

INGREDIENTS

Serves 4

12 quail eggs
2 tablespoons vegetable oil
4 shallots or 1 medium onion, finely chopped
1-inch piece fresh galangal or ginger, chopped
2 garlic cloves, crushed
2-inch piece lemongrass, shredded
1–2 small, fresh red chilies, seeded and finely chopped
¼ teaspoon ground turmeric
½-inch square shrimp paste or 1 tablespoon fish sauce
2 pounds jumbo shrimp, peeled and deveined
1⅔ cups coconut milk
1¼ cups chicken broth
4 ounces Chinese cabbage, roughly shredded
2 teaspoons sugar
salt
2 scallions, green parts only, cut into fine strips, and 2 tablespoons shredded fresh coconut, to garnish

1 Put the quail eggs in a saucepan, cover with water and boil for 8 minutes. Refresh in cold water, peel by dipping in cold water to release the shells and set aside.

2 Heat the oil in a preheated wok. Add the shallots or onion, galangal or ginger and garlic and stir-fry for 1 minute, or until soft but not colored. Add the lemongrass, chilies, turmeric and shrimp paste or fish sauce and stir-fry for 1 minute.

3 Add the shrimp to the wok and stir-fry for 1 minute. Strain the coconut milk and add the thin liquid to the wok, together with the chicken broth. Add the Chinese cabbage and sugar and season to taste with salt. Bring to a boil, reduce the heat and simmer for 6 to 8 minutes.

4 Turn the curry out onto a serving dish. Halve the quail eggs and toss them in the sauce. Scatter the scallions and shredded coconut on top and serve immediately.

COOK'S TIP

Quail eggs are available from specialty grocers and delicatessens. If you cannot find them, use hen eggs—one hen egg is the equivalent of four quail eggs.

Ragout of Shellfish with Sweet-Scented Basil

Green curry paste, so called because it is made with green chilies, is an essential part of Thai cuisine. It can be used to accompany many other dishes and will keep for up to three weeks in the refrigerator. Ready-made curry pastes are available, but they are not as full of flavor as the homemade variety.

Ingredients

Serves 4–6

1 pound mussels in their shells
¼ cup water
8 ounces medium squid
1⅓ cups coconut milk
1¼ cups chicken or vegetable broth
12 ounces monkfish or red snapper, skinned
5 ounces raw or cooked jumbo shrimp, peeled and deveined
4 scallops, shelled and sliced
3 ounces green beans, trimmed and cooked
2 ounces canned bamboo shoots, drained
1 tomato, skinned, seeded and roughly chopped
4 sprigs large-leaf basil, torn, to garnish
boiled rice, to serve

For the green curry paste

2 teaspoons coriander seeds
½ teaspoon caraway or cumin seeds
3–4 medium fresh green chilies, finely chopped
4 teaspoons sugar
2 teaspoons salt
3-inch piece lemongrass
¾-inch piece fresh galangal or ginger, peeled and finely chopped
3 garlic cloves, crushed
4 shallots or 1 medium onion, finely chopped
¾-inch square shrimp paste
2 ounces fresh cilantro leaves, finely chopped
3 tablespoons finely chopped fresh basil
½ teaspoon grated nutmeg
2 tablespoons vegetable oil

1 Scrub the mussels in cold running water and pull off the "beards." Discard any that do not shut when sharply tapped. Put them in a saucepan with the water, cover and cook for 6–8 minutes. Discard any mussels that remain closed and remove three-quarters of the mussels from their shells. Set aside. Strain the cooking liquid and set aside.

2 To prepare the squid, trim off the tentacles and discard the gut. Remove the cuttle shell from inside the body and rub off the skin. Cut the body open and score in a crisscross pattern with a sharp knife. Cut into strips and set aside.

3 To make the green curry paste, dry-fry the coriander and caraway or cumin seeds in a wok. Grind the chilies with the sugar and salt in a mortar with a pestle or in a food processor. Add the coriander and caraway or cumin seeds, lemongrass, galangal or ginger, garlic and shallots or onion and grind. Add the shrimp paste, fresh cilantro, chopped basil, nutmeg and oil and combine thoroughly.

4 Strain the coconut milk and pour the thin liquid into a wok with the chicken or vegetable broth and the reserved cooking liquid from the mussels. Reserve the thick part of the coconut milk. Add 4–5 tablespoons of the green curry paste to the wok and bring the mixture to a boil. Boil rapidly for a few minutes, until the liquid has reduced completely.

5 Add the thick part of the coconut milk, then add the squid and monkfish or red snapper. Simmer for 15–20 minutes. Then add the shrimp, scallops, mussels, beans, bamboo shoots and tomato. Simmer for 2–3 minutes, or until cooked through. Transfer to a warmed serving dish, garnish with torn basil leaves and serve immediately with boiled rice.

Battered Fish, Shrimp and Vegetables

This is a recipe for tempura, one of the few dishes that was brought to Japan from the West. The idea came from Spanish and Portuguese missionaries who settled in southern Japan in the late sixteenth century.

INGREDIENTS

Serves 4-6
1 sheet nori
8 large jumbo shrimp
6 ounces monkfish fillet, cut into
  fingers
1 small eggplant
4 scallions, trimmed
6 fresh shiitake mushrooms
vegetable oil, for deep-frying
flour, for dusting
salt
5 tablespoons soy or tamari sauce,
  to serve

For the batter
2 egg yolks
1¼ cups ice water
2 cups flour
½ teaspoon salt

1 Cut the nori into strips ½ inch wide and 2 inches long. Moisten one end of each strip with water and wrap it round the tail end of each shrimp. Skewer the shrimp along their length to straighten them. Skewer the fingers of monkfish and set aside.

2 Slice the eggplant into neat sections, sprinkle with salt and arrange in layers on a plate. Press lightly with your hand to expel the bitter juices, then leave for 20–30 minutes. Rinse thoroughly under cold water, dry well and thread onto bamboo skewers. Thread the scallions and shiitake mushrooms onto skewers.

3 Make the batter just before using. Beat together the egg yolks and half the ice water. Sift in the flour and salt and stir lightly with chopsticks without mixing to a dry paste. Add the remaining water and stir to make a smooth batter. Avoid overmixing.

4 Heat the oil to 350°F in a wok fitted with a wire draining rack. Dust the skewered vegetables and fish in flour. Dip them into the batter to coat, then fry, not more than three at a time, for 1–2 minutes, or until crisp and golden. Drain well, sprinkle with salt and drain on paper towels. Serve with soy or tamari sauce for dipping.

Shrimp Satés

For *Saté Udang*, jumbo shrimp look spectacular and taste wonderful. The spicy coconut marinade marries beautifully with the shrimp and is also excellent when used with firm cubes of monkfish or halibut and cooked in the same way.

INGREDIENTS

Makes 4 skewers
12 uncooked jumbo shrimp

For the marinade
¼ teaspoon shrimp paste
1 garlic clove, crushed
1 lemon grass stem, lower 2½ inches
   sliced, top reserved
3–4 macadamia nuts or 6–8 almonds
½ teaspoon chili powder
salt
oil for frying
8 tablespoons coconut milk
½ teaspoon tamarind pulp, soaked in
   2 tablespoons water, then strained
   and juice reserved

To serve
Peanut Sauce
cucumber cubes (optional)
lemon wedges

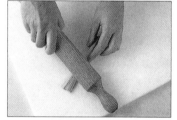

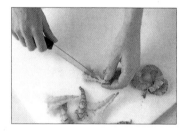

1 Remove the heads from the shrimp. Peel the shrimp and remove the black cord, if liked. Using a small sharp knife, make an incision along the underbody of each shrimp, without cutting it completely in half and open it up like a book. Thread 3 of the shrimp onto each skewer.

2 Make the marinade. Grind the shrimp paste, garlic, lemon grass slices, nuts, chili powder and a little salt to a paste in a food processor or with a mortar and pestle.

3 Fry the paste in oil for 1 minute. Add the coconut milk and tamarind juice. Simmer for 1 minute. Cool. Pour over the shrimp and leave for 1 hour.

4 Cook the shrimp under a hot broiler or on the barbecue grill for 3 minutes or until cooked through. Beat the top part of the lemon grass with the end of a rolling pin, to make it into a brush. Use this to brush the shrimp with the marinade during cooking.

5 Serve on a platter, with the Peanut Sauce, cucumber cubes, if using, and lemon wedges.

Shrimp with Chayote in Turmeric Sauce

This delicious, attractively colored dish is called *Gule Udang Dengan Labu Kuning*.

INGREDIENTS

Serves 4
1–2 chayotes or 2–3 zucchini
2 fresh red chilies, seeded
1 onion, quartered
¼ inch fresh *laos*, peeled
1 lemon grass stem, lower 2 inches
    sliced, top bruised
1 inch fresh turmeric, peeled
⅞ cup water
lemon juice
14-ounce can coconut milk
1 pound cooked, peeled shrimp
salt
red chili shreds, to garnish (optional)
boiled rice, to serve

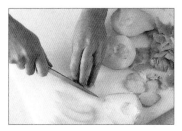

1 Peel the chayotes, remove the seeds and cut into strips. If using zucchini, cut into 2-inch strips.

2 Grind the fresh red chilies, onion, sliced *laos*, sliced lemon grass and the fresh turmeric to a paste in a food processor or with a mortar and pestle. Add the water to the paste mixture, with a squeeze of lemon juice and salt to taste.

3 Pour into a pan. Add the top of the lemon grass stem. Bring to the boil and cook for 1–2 minutes. Add the chayote or zucchini pieces and cook for 2 minutes. Stir in the coconut milk. Taste and adjust the seasoning.

4 Stir in the shrimp and cook gently for 2–3 minutes. Remove the lemon grass stem. Garnish with shreds of chili, if using, and serve with rice.

Doedoeh of Fish

Haddock or cod fillet may be substituted in this recipe.

INGREDIENTS

Serves 6–8
2¼ pounds fresh mackerel
    fillets, skinned
2 tablespoons tamarind pulp, soaked in
    ⅞ cup water
1 onion
½ inch fresh *laos*
2 garlic cloves
1–2 fresh red chilies, seeded, or
    1 teaspoon chili powder
1 teaspoon ground coriander
1 teaspoon ground turmeric
⅓ teaspoon ground fennel seeds
1 tablespoon dark brown sugar
6–7 tablespoons oil
⅞ cup coconut cream
salt and freshly ground black pepper
fresh chili shreds, to garnish

1 Rinse the fish fillets in cold water and dry them well on paper towels. Put into a shallow dish and sprinkle with a little salt. Strain the tamarind and pour the juice over the fish fillets. Set aside for 30 minutes.

2 Quarter the onion, peel and slice the *laos* and peel the garlic. Grind the onion, *laos*, garlic and chilies or chili powder to a paste in a food processor or with a mortar and pestle. Add the ground coriander, turmeric, fennel seeds and sugar.

3 Heat half of the oil in a frying pan. Drain the fish fillets and fry for 5 minutes, or until cooked. Set aside.

4 Wipe out the pan and heat the remaining oil. Fry the spice paste, stirring constantly, until it gives off a spicy aroma. Do not let it brown. Add the coconut cream and simmer gently for a few minutes. Add the fish fillets and gently heat through.

5 Taste for seasoning and serve sprinkled with shredded chili.

Red and White Shrimp with Green Vegetables

The Chinese name for this dish is *Yuan Yang* shrimp. Pairs of mandarin ducks are also known as *yuan yang*, or love birds, because they are always seen together. They symbolize affection and happiness.

INGREDIENTS

Serves 4–6

1 pound jumbo shrimp
½ egg white
1 tablespoon cornstarch paste
6 ounces snow peas
about 2½ cups vegetable oil
1 teaspoon light brown sugar
1 tablespoon finely chopped scallion
1 teaspoon finely chopped fresh ginger
1 tablespoon light soy sauce
1 tablespoon Chinese rice wine or
  dry sherry
1 teaspoon chili bean sauce
1 tablespoon tomato paste
salt

1 Peel and devein the shrimp and mix with the egg white, cornstarch paste and a pinch of salt. Trim the snow peas.

2 Heat 2–3 tablespoons of the oil in a preheated wok and stir-fry the snow peas for about 1 minute. Add the sugar and a little salt and continue stirring for 1 more minute. Remove and place in the center of a warmed serving platter.

3 Add the remaining oil to the wok and cook the shrimp for 1 minute. Remove and drain.

4 Pour off all but about 1 tablespoon of the oil. Add the scallion and ginger to the wok.

5 Return the shrimp to the wok and stir-fry for 1 minute, then add the soy sauce and rice wine or dry sherry. Blend the mixture thoroughly. Transfer half the shrimp to one end of the serving platter.

6 Add the chili bean sauce and tomato paste to the remaining shrimp in the wok, blend well and place the "red" shrimp at the other end of the platter. Serve.

COOK'S TIP

All raw shrimp have an intestinal tract that runs just beneath the outside curve of the tail. The tract is not poisonous, but it can taste unpleasant. It is therefore best to remove it, or "devein." To do this, peel the shrimp, leaving the tail intact. Score each shrimp lightly along its length to expose the tract. Remove the tract with a small knife or Chinese cleaver.

Vietnamese Stuffed Squid

The smaller the squid, the sweeter the dish will taste. Be very careful not to overcook the flesh, as it becomes tough extremely quickly.

INGREDIENTS

Serves 4
8 small squid
2 ounces cellophane noodles
2 tablespoons peanut oil
2 scallions, finely chopped
8 shiitake mushrooms, halved if large
9 ounces ground pork
1 garlic clove, chopped
2 tablespoons fish sauce
1 teaspoon superfine sugar
1 tablespoon finely chopped fresh
  cilantro
1 teaspoon lemon juice
salt and freshly ground black pepper

1 Cut off the tentacles of the squid just below the eye. Remove the transparent "quill" from inside the body and rub off the skin on the outside. Wash thoroughly in cold water and set aside.

2 Bring a saucepan of water to a boil and add the noodles. Remove from the heat and set aside to soak for 20 minutes.

3 Heat 1 tablespoon of the oil in a preheated wok and stir-fry the scallions, shiitake mushrooms, pork and garlic for 4 minutes, or until the meat is golden.

4 Drain the noodles and add to the wok, with the fish sauce, sugar, cilantro, lemon juice and salt and pepper to taste.

5 Stuff the squid with the mixture and secure with toothpicks or satay sticks. Arrange the squid in an ovenproof dish, drizzle with the remaining oil, and prick each squid twice. Bake in a preheated oven at 400°F for 10 minutes. Serve hot.

Stir-fried Five-Spice Squid

Squid is perfect for stir-frying, as it should be cooked quickly. The spicy sauce makes the ideal accompaniment.

INGREDIENTS

Serves 6

1 pound small squid, cleaned
3 tablespoons oil
1-inch piece fresh ginger, grated
1 garlic clove, crushed
8 scallions, cut diagonally into
    1-inch lengths
1 red bell pepper, seeded and cut into
    strips
1 fresh green chili, seeded and sliced
6 mushrooms, sliced
1 teaspoon Chinese five-spice powder
2 tablespoons black bean sauce
2 tablespoons soy sauce
1 teaspoon sugar
1 tablespoon Chinese rice wine or
    dry sherry

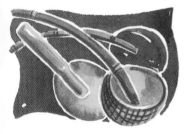

1 Rinse the squid and pull away and discard the outer skin. Dry on paper towels. Slit the squid open and score the inside into diamonds with a sharp knife. Cut the squid into strips.

2 Heat the oil in a preheated wok. Stir-fry the squid quickly. Remove the squid strips from the wok with a slotted spoon and set aside. Add the ginger, garlic, scallions, red bell pepper, chili and mushrooms to the oil remaining in the wok and stir-fry for 2 minutes.

3 Return the squid to the wok and stir in the five-spice powder. Stir in the black bean sauce, soy sauce, sugar and rice wine or dry sherry. Bring to a boil and cook, stirring, for 1 minute. Serve immediately.

Clay Pot of Chili Squid and Noodles

INGREDIENTS

Serves 4

1½ pounds fresh squid
2 tablespoons vegetable oil
3 slices fresh ginger,
  finely shredded
2 garlic cloves, finely chopped
1 red onion, finely sliced
1 carrot, finely sliced
1 celery stalk, diagonally sliced
2 ounces sugar snap peas,
  ends removed
1 teaspoon sugar
1 tablespoon chili bean paste
½ teaspoon chili powder
3 ounces cellophane noodles, soaked
  in hot water until soft
⅓ cup chicken broth
  or water
1 tablespoon soy sauce
1 tablespoon oyster sauce
1 teaspoon sesame oil
pinch of salt
cilantro leaves, to garnish

1 Prepare the squid. Holding the body in one hand, gently pull away the head and tentacles. Discard the head; trim and reserve the tentacles. Remove the transparent "quill" from inside the body of the squid. Peel off the brown skin on the outside of the body. Rub a little salt into the squid, and wash thoroughly under cold running water. Cut the body of the squid into rings or split it open lengthwise, score crisscross patterns on the inside of the body, and cut it into 2-inch x 1½-inch pieces.

2 Heat the oil in a large clay pot or flameproof casserole. Add the ginger, garlic and onion, and fry for 1–2 minutes. Add the squid, carrot, celery and peas. Fry until the squid curls up. Season with salt and sugar, and stir in the chili bean paste and powder. Transfer the mixture to a bowl, and set aside until required.

3 Drain the soaked noodles, and add them to the clay pot or casserole. Stir in the broth or water, soy sauce and oyster sauce. Cover, and cook over a medium heat for about 10 minutes or until the noodles are tender.

4 Return the squid and vegetables to the pot. Cover, and cook for about 5–6 minutes more, until all the flavors are combined. Season to taste.

5 Just before serving, drizzle with the sesame oil, and sprinkle with the cilantro leaves.

--- COOK'S TIP ---

These noodles have a smooth, light texture that readily absorbs the other flavors in the dish. To vary the flavor, the vegetables can be altered according to what is available.

Squid with Bell Pepper and Black Bean Sauce

This dish is a product of the Cantonese school. It makes an attractive meal that is just as delicious as it looks.

INGREDIENTS

Serves 4

12–14 ounces squid
1 medium green bell pepper, cored
3–4 tablespoons vegetable oil
1 garlic clove, finely chopped
½ teaspoon finely chopped fresh ginger
1 tablespoon finely chopped scallion
1 teaspoon salt
1 tablespoon black bean sauce
1 tablespoon Chinese rice wine or
  dry sherry
few drops of sesame oil

1 To clean the squid, cut off the tentacles just below the eye. Remove the "quill" from inside the body. Peel off and discard the skin, then wash the squid and dry well. Cut open the squid and score the inside of the flesh in a crisscross pattern.

2 Cut the squid into pieces each about the size of an oblong postage stamp. Blanch the squid in a pan of boiling water for a few seconds. Remove and drain. Dry well.

3 Cut the green bell pepper into small triangular pieces. Heat the oil in a preheated wok and stir-fry the bell pepper for about 1 minute.

4 Add the garlic, ginger, scallion, salt and squid, then stir for 1 minute. Add the black bean sauce, rice wine or dry sherry and sesame oil and serve.

MEAT

Satisfying beef curries, quick and easy stir-fried steak, fragrant lamb dishes and, of course, sweet-and-sour pork—the range of Chinese and other Asian meat recipes is immense, offering something special for all tastes and budgets. The recipes in this chapter include inexpensive and easy-to-prepare weekday family meals, such as Braised Beef in a Rich Peanut Sauce and Pork and Vegetable Stir-fry, as well as impressive and unusual dinner party dishes, such as Beef and Vegetables in a Tabletop Broth and Braised Birthday Noodles with Hoisin Lamb.

Peking Beef and Bell Pepper Stir-fry

This quick and easy stir-fry is
perfect for today's busy cook and
tastes superb.

INGREDIENTS

Serves 4

12 ounces sirloin steak, sliced into strips
2 tablespoons soy sauce
2 tablespoons medium sherry
1 tablespoon cornstarch
1 teaspoon light brown sugar
1 tablespoon sunflower oil
1 tablespoon sesame oil
1 garlic clove, finely chopped
1 tablespoon grated fresh ginger
1 red bell pepper, seeded and sliced
1 yellow bell pepper, seeded and sliced
4 ounces sugar snap peas
4 scallions, cut into 2-inch lengths
2 tablespoons oyster sauce
4 tablespoons water
cooked noodles, to serve

1 In a bowl, mix together the steak
strips, soy sauce, sherry, cornstarch,
and brown sugar. Cover and marinate
for 30 minutes.

2 Heat the sunflower and sesame oils
in a preheated wok or large frying
pan. Add the garlic and ginger and stir-
fry for about 30 seconds. Add the bell
peppers, sugar snap peas and scallions
and stir-fry for 3 minutes.

3 Add the beef, together with the
marinade juices, to the wok or
frying pan and stir-fry for another
3–4 minutes. Pour in the oyster sauce
and water and stir until the sauce has
thickened slightly. Serve immediately
with cooked noodles.

Stir-fried Beef and Broccoli

This spicy beef may be served with noodles or on a bed of boiled rice for a speedy and low-calorie Chinese meal.

INGREDIENTS

Serves 4

12 ounces sirloin steak
1 tablespoon cornstarch
1 teaspoon sesame oil
12 ounces broccoli, cut into small florets
4 scallions, sliced diagonally
1 medium carrot, cut into short thin sticks
1 garlic clove, crushed
1-inch piece fresh ginger, cut into very fine strips
½ cup beef broth
2 tablespoons soy sauce
2 tablespoons dry sherry
2 teaspoons light brown sugar
scallion tassels, to garnish (optional)
noodles or rice, to serve

1 Trim the beef and cut into thin slices across the grain. Cut each slice into thin strips. Toss in the cornstarch to coat thoroughly.

2 Heat the sesame oil in a preheated wok or large nonstick frying pan. Add the beef strips and stir-fry for 3 minutes. Remove and set aside.

3 Add the broccoli, scallions, carrot, garlic, ginger and broth to the wok or frying pan. Cover and simmer for 3 minutes. Uncover and cook, stirring, until the broth has reduced entirely.

4 Combine the soy sauce, dry sherry and brown sugar together and add to the wok or frying pan with the beef. Cook for 2–3 minutes or until it is cooked, stirring continuously. Spoon into a warmed serving dish and garnish with scallion tassels, if desired. Serve on a bed of noodles or rice.

COOK'S TIP

To make scallion tassels, trim the bulb base, then cut the green shoot so that the onion is 3 inches long. Shred to within 1 inch of the base and put into ice water for 1 hour.

Beef Stir-fry with Crisp Parsnips

Wonderful crisp shreds of parsnip add extra crunchiness to this unusual stir-fry—a great supper dish to share with friends.

INGREDIENTS

Serves 4

12 ounces parsnips
1 pound sirloin steak
1 pound trimmed leeks
2 red bell peppers, seeded
12 ounces zucchini
6 tablespoons vegetable oil
2 garlic cloves, crushed
3 tablespoons hoisin sauce
salt and freshly ground black pepper

2 Cut the steak into thin strips. Split the leeks in half lengthwise and thickly slice at an angle. Roughly chop the bell peppers and thinly slice the zucchini.

5 Stir-fry the garlic, leeks, bell peppers and zucchini for about 10 minutes, or until golden brown and beginning to soften but still retaining a little bite. Season the mixture well.

1 Peel the parsnips and cut in half lengthwise. Place the halves flat surface down on a cutting board and cut them into thin strips. Finely shred each piece. Rinse in cold water and drain thoroughly. Dry the parsnips on paper towels, if necessary.

3 Heat the oil in a preheated wok or large frying pan. Fry the parsnips until crisp and golden. You may need to do this in batches, adding a little more oil if necessary. Remove with a slotted spoon and drain on paper towels.

6 Return the meat to the pan with the hoisin sauce. Stir-fry for 2–3 minutes, or until piping hot. Adjust the seasoning and serve with the crisp parsnips piled on top.

4 Stir-fry the steak in the wok or frying pan until golden and cooked through. You may need to do this in batches, adding more oil if necessary. Remove and drain on paper towels.

Beef with Cantonese Oyster Sauce

This is a classic Cantonese recipe in which any combination of vegetables can be used. Broccoli may be used instead of snow peas, bamboo shoots instead of baby corn, and white or black mushrooms instead of straw mushrooms, for example.

INGREDIENTS

Serves 4
10–12 ounces sirloin steak
1 teaspoon light brown sugar
1 tablespoon light soy sauce
2 teaspoons Chinese rice wine or
 dry sherry
2 teaspoons cornstarch paste
4 ounces snow peas
4 ounces baby corn
4 ounces straw mushrooms
1 scallion
1¼ cups vegetable oil
few small pieces of fresh ginger
½ teaspoon salt
2 tablespoons oyster sauce

1 Cut the beef into thin strips. Place in a bowl and add the sugar, soy sauce, rice wine or dry sherry and cornstarch paste. Mix well and marinate for 25–30 minutes.

2 Trim the snow peas and cut the baby corn in half. If using canned straw mushrooms, drain them. If the straw mushrooms are large, cut them in half, but leave whole if they are small. Cut the scallion into short sections.

3 Heat the oil in a preheated wok and stir-fry the beef until the color changes. Remove with a slotted spoon and drain.

4 Pour off the excess oil, leaving about 2 tablespoons in the wok, then add the scallion, ginger and vegetables. Stir-fry for about 2 minutes with the salt, then add the beef and the oyster sauce. Blend well and serve.

Beef Strips with Orange and Ginger

Stir-frying is one of the best ways to cook with the minimum of fat. This recipe is ideal for people trying to lose weight, those requiring a low-fat and low-cholesterol diet or, in fact, anyone who wants to eat healthfully.

INGREDIENTS

Serves 4
1 pound lean sirloin steak, cut into thin strips
finely grated rind and juice of 1 orange
1 tablespoon light soy sauce
1 teaspoon cornstarch
1-inch piece fresh ginger, chopped
2 teaspoons sesame oil
1 large carrot, cut into short thin sticks
2 scallions, thinly sliced
rice noodles or boiled rice, to serve

1 Place the steak strips in a bowl and sprinkle with the orange rind and juice. Marinate for about 30 minutes.

2 Drain the liquid from the steak and reserve it. Combine the steak, soy sauce, cornstarch and ginger.

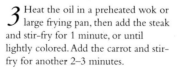

3 Heat the oil in a preheated wok or large frying pan, then add the steak and stir-fry for 1 minute, or until lightly colored. Add the carrot and stir-fry for another 2–3 minutes.

4 Stir in the scallions and reserved marinade liquid. Cook, stirring constantly, until boiling and thickened. Serve hot with rice noodles or plain boiled rice.

Sizzling Steak

This Malaysian method of sizzling richly marinated meat on a cast-iron grill can be applied with equal success to sliced chicken or pork.

INGREDIENTS

Serves 4–6

1 garlic clove, crushed
1-inch piece fresh ginger, finely chopped
2 teaspoons black peppercorns
1 tablespoon sugar
2 tablespoons tamarind sauce
3 tablespoons dark soy sauce
1 tablespoon oyster sauce
4 slices sirloin steak, each about 7 ounces
vegetable oil, for brushing
shredded scallions and carrot, to garnish

For the dipping sauce

5 tablespoons beef broth
2 tablespoons ketchup
1 teaspoon chili sauce
juice of 1 lime

1 Pound together the garlic, ginger, peppercorns, sugar and tamarind sauce in a mortar with a pestle. Mix in the soy sauce and oyster sauce, then spoon over the steaks. Marinate in the refrigerator for up to 8 hours.

2 Heat a cast-iron grill over high heat until very hot. Scrape the marinade from the meat into a saucepan and reserve. Brush the meat with oil and grill for 2 minutes on each side for rare and 3–4 minutes on each side for medium, depending on thickness.

3 Meanwhile, make the sauce. Add the beef broth, ketchup, chili sauce and lime juice to the marinade. Set over low heat and simmer to heat through. Garnish the steak with scallions and carrot and serve. Pass the dipping sauce separately.

Thick Beef Curry in Sweet Peanut Sauce

This curry is deliciously rich and thicker than most other Thai curries. Serve it with boiled jasmine rice and salted duck's eggs, if you like.

INGREDIENTS

Serves 4–6
2½ cups unsweetened coconut milk
3 tablespoons red curry paste
3 tablespoons fish sauce
2 tablespoons palm sugar
2 lemongrass stalks, bruised
1 pound sirloin steak, cut into
   thin strips
¾ cup roasted ground peanuts
2 red chilies, sliced
5 kaffir lime leaves, torn
salt and freshly ground black pepper
2 salted eggs, to serve
10–15 Thai basil leaves, to garnish

1 Put half the coconut milk into a heavy-bottomed saucepan and heat, stirring, until it boils and separates.

--- COOK'S TIP ---

If you don't have the time to make your own red curry paste, you can buy a ready-made Thai curry paste. There is a wide range available in most supermarkets.

2 Add the red curry paste and cook until fragrant. Add the fish sauce, palm sugar and lemongrass.

3 Continue to cook until the color deepens. Add the rest of the coconut milk. Bring back to a boil.

4 Add the beef and ground peanuts. Stir and cook for 8–10 minutes or until most of the liquid has evaporated.

5 Add the chilies and kaffir lime leaves. Adjust the seasoning to taste. Serve with salted eggs and garnish with Thai basil leaves.

Sesame Steak

Toasted sesame seeds bring their distinctive smoky aroma to this scrumptious Asian marinade.

INGREDIENTS

Serves 4

1 pound sirloin steak
2 tablespoons sesame seeds
1 tablespoon sesame oil
2 tablespoons vegetable oil
4 ounces small mushrooms, quartered
1 large green bell pepper, seeded and
    cut into strips
4 scallions, chopped diagonally
boiled rice, to serve

For the marinade

2 teaspoons cornstarch
2 tablespoons Chinese rice wine or
    dry sherry
1 tablespoon lemon juice
1 tablespoon soy sauce
few drops of Tabasco sauce
1-inch piece fresh ginger, grated
1 garlic clove, crushed

1 Trim the steak and cut into thin strips about ½ x 2 inch.

2 Make the marinade. In a bowl, blend the cornstarch with the rice wine or dry sherry, then stir in the lemon juice, soy sauce, Tabasco sauce, ginger and garlic. Stir in the steak strips, cover and leave in a cool place for 3–4 hours.

3 Place the sesame seeds in a wok or large frying pan and dry-fry over moderate heat, shaking the pan, until the seeds are golden. Set aside.

4 Heat the sesame and vegetable oils in the wok or frying pan. Drain the steak, reserving the marinade, and stir-fry a few pieces at a time until browned. Remove with a slotted spoon.

5 Add the mushrooms and green bell pepper and stir-fry for 2–3 minutes. Add the scallions and cook for 1 minute more.

6 Return the steak to the wok or frying pan, together with the reserved marinade, and stir over a moderate heat for a further 2 minutes, or until the ingredients are evenly coated with glaze. Sprinkle the sesame seeds on top and serve immediately with boiled rice.

COOK'S TIP

This marinade would also be good with pork or chicken.

Stir-fried Beef with Snow Peas

The crisp texture and fresh taste of snow peas perfectly complement the melt-in-the-mouth tenderness of the steak, all served in a richly aromatic sauce.

INGREDIENTS

Serves 4
1 pound sirloin steak
3 tablespoons soy sauce
2 tablespoons Chinese rice wine or
   dry sherry
1 tablespoon light brown sugar
½ teaspoon cornstarch
1 tablespoon vegetable oil
1 tablespoon finely chopped fresh
   ginger
1 tablespoon finely chopped garlic
8 ounces snow peas

1 Cut the steak into even-sized, very thin strips.

2 Combine the soy sauce, rice wine or dry sherry, sugar and cornstarch. Mix well and set aside.

3 Heat the oil in a preheated wok. Add the ginger and garlic and stir-fry for 30 seconds. Add the steak and stir-fry for 2 minutes, or until evenly browned.

4 Add the snow peas and stir-fry for another 3 minutes.

5 Stir the soy sauce mixture until smooth, then add to the wok. Bring to a boil, stirring constantly, lower the heat and simmer until the sauce is thick and smooth. Serve immediately.

Braised Beef in a Rich Peanut Sauce

Like many dishes brought to the Philippines by the Spanish, this slow-cooking stew, renamed *Kari Kari*, retains much of its original charm, while at the same time it has acquired a uniquely Asian flavor. Rice and peanuts are used to thicken the juices, yielding a rich, glossy sauce.

INGREDIENTS

Serves 4–6
2 pounds chuck steak
2 tablespoons vegetable oil
1 tablespoon annatto seeds
2 medium onions, chopped
2 garlic cloves, crushed
10 ounces celery root or rutabaga
   roughly chopped
2 cups beef broth
12 ounces new potatoes, peeled and cut
   into large dice
1 tablespoon fish or anchovy sauce
2 tablespoons tamarind sauce
2 teaspoons sugar
1 bay leaf
1 fresh thyme sprig
3 tablespoons long-grain rice
½ cup peanuts or 2 tablespoons peanut
   butter
1 tablespoon white wine vinegar
salt and freshly ground black pepper

1 Cut the beef into 1-inch cubes and set aside. Heat the oil in a flameproof casserole, add the annatto seeds and stir until the oil is dark red in color. Remove the seeds with a slotted spoon and discard.

2 Add the onions, garlic and celery root or rutabaga to the casserole and fry for 3–5 minutes, or until softened but not colored. Add the beef and fry until lightly and evenly browned. Add the broth, potatoes, fish or anchovy sauce, tamarind sauce, sugar, bay leaf and thyme. Bring to a simmer, cover and cook for 2 hours.

3 Meanwhile, place the rice in a bowl, cover with cold water and set aside for 30 minutes. Roast the peanuts, if using, under a preheated broiler for 2 minutes. Remove and rub off the skins with a clean kitchen towel. Drain the rice and grind with the peanuts or peanut butter in a mortar with a pestle or in a food processor.

4 When the beef is tender, add 4 tablespoons of the cooking liquid to the rice and nut mixture. Blend until smooth, then stir into the casserole. Simmer gently, uncovered, for 15–20 minutes, or until thickened. Stir in the wine vinegar and season to taste.

COOK'S TIP

Annatto seeds have little flavor, although they are edible. They are used to color oil or shortening to a rich reddish-orange shade. If you cannot find them, substitute 1 teaspoon paprika and a pinch of turmeric, adding these to the casserole with the beef.

Beef and Vegetables in a Tabletop Broth

In Japanese, this dish is called *Shabu Shabu*, which refers to the swishing sound made as wafer-thin slices of beef, tofu and vegetables cook in a special broth. This is a delicious and easy all-in-one main course for a dinner party.

INGREDIENTS

Serves 4–6
1 pound sirloin steak, trimmed
7½ cups water
½ packet instant dashi powder or
½ vegetable bouillon cube
2 large carrots
6 scallions, sliced
5 ounces Chinese cabbage, roughly chopped
8 ounces daikon, cut into thin strips
1 can (4 ounces) bamboo shoots, drained and sliced (optional)
6 ounces firm tofu, cut into large dice
10 shiitake mushrooms, fresh or dried
salt
10 ounces udon noodles, cooked, to serve

For the sesame dipping sauce
2 ounces sesame seeds or 2 tablespoons tahini paste
½ cup instant dashi broth or vegetable broth
4 tablespoons dark soy sauce
2 teaspoons sugar
2 tablespoons sake (optional)
2 teaspoons wasabi powder (optional)

For the ponzu dipping sauce
3 tablespoons lemon juice
1 tablespoon rice vinegar or white wine vinegar
3 tablespoons dark soy sauce
1 tablespoon tamari sauce
1 tablespoon mirin or 1 teaspoon sugar
¼ teaspoon instant dashi powder or
¼ vegetable bouillon cube

1 Place the beef in the freezer for 30 minutes, or until firm but not frozen. Slice it very thinly using a cleaver or large, sharp knife. Arrange it decoratively on a serving plate, cover and set aside. Bring the water to a boil in a Japanese *donabe*, a fondue pot or any other covered flameproof casserole with an unglazed outside. Stir in the *dashi* powder or bouillon cube, cover and simmer for 8–10 minutes. Transfer the container to a heat source (its own stand or a hot plate) at the dining table.

2 Meanwhile, prepare the vegetables and bring a saucepan of lightly salted water to a boil. With a paring knife, cut a series of grooves along the length of the carrots, then slice thinly. Blanch the carrots, scallions, Chinese cabbage and daikon, separately, for 2–3 minutes each and drain thoroughly. Arrange the vegetables decoratively on serving plates, together with the bamboo shoots and tofu. If using dried shiitake mushrooms, put them in a bowl, cover with hot water and soak for 3–4 minutes, then drain. Slice the mushrooms.

3 To make the sesame dipping sauce, dry-fry the sesame seeds, if using, in a heavy frying pan over medium heat. Grind them in a mortar with a pestle or in a food processor.

4 Combine the ground sesame seeds or tahini paste, broth, soy sauce, sugar, sake and wasabi powder, if using. Combine thoroughly and pour into a shallow dish.

5 To make the ponzu dipping sauce, put all the ingredients in a screw-top jar and shake vigorously. Pour into a shallow dish.

6 To serve, arrange the plates of vegetables and dishes of sauce around the *donabe*, fondue pot or flameproof casserole, and provide your guests with chopsticks and individual bowls so that they can help themselves to what they want, cook it in the broth and then serve themselves. Toward the end of the meal, each guest can take a portion of noodles and ladle a little stock over them before eating.

COOK'S TIP

Tahini paste is a purée of toasted sesame seeds that is used mainly in Greek, Turkish and some Middle Eastern cooking. It makes a quick alternative to using sesame seeds in this recipe and is readily available from large supermarkets and delicatessens.

Sukiyaki Beef

This Japanese dish, with its mixture of meat, vegetables, noodles and tofu, is a meal in itself. If you want to do it properly, eat the meal with chopsticks and then use a spoon to collect the broth.

INGREDIENTS

Serves 4
1 pound thick sirloin steak
7 ounces Japanese rice noodles
1 tablespoon shredded suet
7 ounces firm tofu, cut into cubes
8 shiitake mushrooms, hard stems trimmed
2 medium leeks, sliced into 1-inch lengths
3½ ounces baby spinach, to serve

For the broth
1 tablespoon superfine sugar
6 tablespoons sake, Chinese rice wine or dry sherry
3 tablespoons dark soy sauce
½ cup water

3 Make the broth: combine the sugar, sake, rice wine or dry sherry, soy sauce and water.

4 Melt the shortening in a preheated wok. Add the steak and stir-fry for 2–3 minutes, or until cooked through but still pink.

5 Pour the broth over the beef.

6 Add the tofu, mushrooms and leeks and cook for 4 minutes, or until the leeks are tender. Serve a selection of the different ingredients, together with a few baby spinach leaves, to each person.

1 Cut the steak into thin slices using a cleaver or sharp knife.

2 Blanch the noodles in boiling water for 2 minutes. Drain thoroughly and set aside.

Beef Saté with Hot Mango Dip

Aromatic beef is served with a
spicy fruit sauce. Just add salad
greens and plain boiled rice for
the perfect balance of flavors and
textures.

INGREDIENTS

Serves 4
1 pound sirloin steak
1 tablespoon coriander seeds
1 teaspoon cumin seeds
½ cup raw cashews
1 tablespoon vegetable oil
2 shallots or 1 small onion, finely
    chopped
½-inch piece fresh ginger, finely
    chopped
1 garlic clove, crushed
2 tablespoons tamarind sauce
2 tablespoons dark soy sauce
2 teaspoons sugar
1 teaspoon rice vinegar or white
    wine vinegar
salad greens, to serve

For the hot mango dip
1 ripe mango
1–2 small fresh red chilies, seeded and
    finely chopped
1 tablespoon fish sauce
juice of 1 lime
2 teaspoons sugar
2 tablespoons chopped fresh cilantro
salt

2 Dry-fry coriander seeds, cumin
seeds and cashews in a preheated
wok until evenly brown. Transfer to a
mortar and crush with a pestle, or crush
finely in a food processor. Combine the
crushed spices and nuts, vegetable oil,
shallots or onion, ginger, garlic,
tamarind sauce, soy sauce, sugar and
vinegar. Spoon this mixture over the
beef and marinate for up to 8 hours.

3 Cook the steak skewers under a
preheated broiler for 6–8 minutes,
turning occasionally to ensure an
even color.

4 Meanwhile, make the mango dip.
Peel the mango and cut the flesh
from the pit. Place in a food processor
with the chilies, fish sauce, lime juice
and sugar and process until smooth. Stir
in the cilantro and season with salt to
taste. Serve the skewers on a bed of
greens; serve the sauce on the side.

1 Slice the beef into long, narrow
strips and thread, zigzag style, onto
12 bamboo skewers. Put them on a flat
plate and set aside.

Paper-thin Lamb with Scallions

Scallions lend a delicious flavor to the lamb in this simple supper dish.

INGREDIENTS

Serves 3–4

1 pound lamb neck fillet
2 tablespoons Chinese rice wine or
    dry sherry
2 teaspoons light soy sauce
½ teaspoon roasted and ground
    Szechuan peppercorns
½ teaspoon salt
½ teaspoon dark brown sugar
4 teaspoons dark soy sauce
1 tablespoon sesame oil
2 tablespoons peanut oil
2 garlic cloves, thinly sliced
2 bunches scallions, cut into
    3-inch lengths
2 tablespoons chopped fresh cilantro

1 Wrap the lamb and place in the freezer for about 1 hour, until just frozen. Cut the meat across the grain into paper-thin slices. Put the lamb slices in a bowl, add 2 teaspoons of the rice wine or dry sherry, the light soy sauce and ground Szechuan peppercorns. Mix well and set aside to marinate for 15–30 minutes.

—— COOK'S TIP ——

Some large supermarkets sell very thinly sliced lean lamb ready for stir-frying, which makes this dish even quicker to prepare.

2 Make the sauce: combine the remaining rice wine or dry sherry, salt, sugar, soy sauce and 2 teaspoons of the sesame oil in a bowl. Set aside.

3 Heat the groundnut oil in a preheated wok. Add the garlic and let it sizzle for a few seconds, then add the lamb. Stir-fry for about 1 minute, or until the lamb is no longer pink. Pour in the sauce and stir briefly to mix.

4 Add the scallions and cilantro and stir-fry for 15–20 seconds, or until the scallions just wilt. The finished dish should be slightly dry in appearance. Serve at once, sprinkled with the remaining sesame oil.

Minted Lamb Stir-fry

Lamb and mint have a long-established partnership that works particularly well in this full-flavored stir-fry. Serve with plenty of crusty bread.

INGREDIENTS

Serves 2

10 ounces lamb neck fillet
2 tablespoons sunflower oil
2 teaspoons sesame oil
1 onion, roughly chopped
2 garlic cloves, crushed
1 fresh red chili, seeded and
    finely chopped
3 ounces green beans, halved
8 ounces fresh spinach
2 tablespoons oyster sauce
2 tablespoons fish sauce
1 tablespoon lemon juice
1 teaspoon superfine sugar
3 tablespoons chopped fresh mint
salt and freshly ground black pepper
fresh mint sprigs, to garnish
crusty bread, to serve

1 Trim the lamb of any excess fat and cut into thin slices. Heat the sunflower and sesame oils in a preheated wok or large frying pan and stir-fry the lamb over high heat until browned. Remove with a slotted spoon and drain on paper towels.

2 Add the onion, garlic and chili to the wok and cook for 2–3 minutes. Add the green beans to the wok and stir-fry for 3 minutes.

3 Stir in the spinach with the browned lamb, oyster sauce, fish sauce, lemon juice and sugar. Stir-fry for another 3–4 minutes, or until the lamb is cooked through.

4 Sprinkle with the chopped mint, season to taste and garnish with mint sprigs. Serve piping hot, with plenty of crusty bread to mop up all the juices.

Stir-fried Lamb with Scallions

This is a classic Beijing "meat and vegetables" recipe, in which the lamb can be replaced with either beef or pork, and the scallions by other strongly flavored vegetables, such as leeks or onions.

INGREDIENTS

Serves 4

12–14 ounces leg of lamb fillet
1 teaspoon light brown sugar
1 tablespoon light soy sauce
1 tablespoon Chinese rice wine or
  dry sherry
2 teaspoons cornstarch paste
½ ounce dried wood ears
6–8 scallions
1¼ cups vegetable oil
few small pieces of fresh ginger
2 tablespoons yellow bean sauce
few drops of sesame oil

2 Heat the oil in a preheated wok and stir-fry the lamb for about 1 minute, or until the color changes. Remove with a slotted spoon, drain and set aside.

3 Pour off all but about 1 tablespoon of the oil from the wok, then add the scallions, ginger, wood ears and yellow bean sauce. Blend well, then add the meat and stir for about 1 minute. Sprinkle with the sesame oil and serve.

1 Slice the lamb thinly and place in a shallow dish. Combine the sugar, soy sauce, rice wine or dry sherry and cornstarch paste, pour over the lamb and marinate for 30–45 minutes. Soak the wood ears in water for 25–30 minutes, then drain and cut into small pieces. Finely chop the scallions.

Five-Spice Lamb

This mouthwatering and aromatic lamb dish is perfect for an informal supper party.

INGREDIENTS

Serves 4

2 tablespoons oil, plus more if needed
3–3½ pounds leg of lamb, boned
   and cubed
1 onion, chopped
2 teaspoons grated fresh ginger
1 garlic clove, crushed
1 teaspoon Chinese five-spice powder
2 tablespoons hoisin sauce
1 tablespoon light soy sauce
1¼ cups tomato paste
1 cup lamb or beef broth
1 red bell pepper, seeded and diced
1 yellow bell pepper, seeded and diced
2 tablespoons chopped fresh cilantro
1 tablespoon sesame seeds, toasted
salt and freshly ground black pepper
boiled rice, to serve

1 Heat the oil in a flameproof casserole and brown the lamb in batches over high heat. Remove and set aside.

2 Add the onion, ginger and garlic to the casserole with a little more oil, if necessary, and cook for about 5 minutes, until softened.

3 Return the lamb to the casserole. Stir in the five-spice powder, hoisin and soy sauces, tomato paste, broth and seasoning. Bring to a boil, cover and cook in a preheated oven at 325°F for 1¼ hours.

4 Remove the casserole from the oven, stir in the bell peppers, then cover and return to the oven for another 15 minutes, or until the lamb is cooked and very tender.

5 Sprinkle with the cilantro and sesame seeds. Serve hot with rice.

Braised Birthday Noodles with Hoisin Lamb

In China, the egg symbolizes continuity and fertility so it is frequently included in birthday dishes. The noodles traditionally served at birthday celebrations are left long: it is considered bad luck to cut them as this might shorten one's life.

INGREDIENTS

Serves 4
12 ounces thick egg noodles
2¼ pounds lamb cutlets
2 tablespoons vegetable oil
4 ounces fine green beans, ends removed and blanched
salt and freshly ground black pepper
2 hard-boiled eggs, halved, and 2 scallions, finely chopped, to garnish

For the marinade
2 garlic cloves, crushed
2 teaspoons grated fresh ginger
2 tablespoons soy sauce
2 tablespoons rice wine
1–2 dried red chilies
2 tablespoons vegetable oil

For the sauce
1 tablespoon cornstarch
2 tablespoons soy sauce
2 tablespoons rice wine
grated rind and juice of ½ orange
1 tablespoon hoisin sauce
1 tablespoon wine vinegar
1 teaspoon light brown sugar

1 Bring a large saucepan of water to a boil. Add the noodles, and cook for 2 minutes only. Drain, rinse under cold water, and drain again. Set aside.

2 Cut the lamb into 2-inch thick medallions. Mix the ingredients for the marinade in a large, shallow dish. Add the lamb, and marinate for at least 4 hours or overnight.

3 Heat the oil in a heavy-bottomed saucepan or flameproof casserole. Fry the lamb for 5 minutes until browned. Add just enough water to cover the meat. Bring to a boil, skim, then reduce the heat, and simmer for 40 minutes or until the meat is tender, adding more water as necessary.

4 Make the sauce. Blend the cornstarch with the remaining ingredients in a bowl. Stir into the lamb, and mix well without breaking up the meat.

5 Add the noodles to the lamb with the beans. Simmer gently until both the noodles and the beans are cooked. Add salt and pepper to taste. Divide the noodles, lamb and beans among four large bowls, garnish each portion with half a hard-cooked egg, sprinkle with scallions and serve.

Pork Chow Mein

A perfect speedy meal, this family favorite is flavored with sesame oil for an authentic Asian taste.

INGREDIENTS

Serves 4

6 ounces medium egg noodles
12 ounces pork fillet
2 tablespoons sunflower oil
1 tablespoon sesame oil
2 garlic cloves, crushed
8 scallions, sliced
1 red bell pepper, seeded and roughly chopped
1 green bell pepper, seeded and roughly chopped
2 tablespoons dark soy sauce
3 tablespoons Chinese rice wine or dry sherry
6 ounces bean sprouts
3 tablespoons chopped flat-leaf parsley
1 tablespoon toasted sesame seeds

1 Soak the noodles according to the package instructions. Drain well.

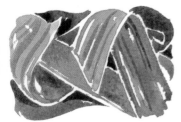

2 Thinly slice the pork fillet. Heat the sunflower oil in a preheated wok or large frying pan and cook the pork over high heat until golden brown and cooked through.

3 Add the sesame oil to the wok or frying pan, with the garlic, scallions and bell peppers. Cook over high heat for 3–4 minutes, or until the vegetables are beginning to soften.

4 Reduce the heat slightly and stir in the noodles, with the soy sauce and rice wine or dry sherry. Stir-fry for 2 minutes. Add the bean sprouts and cook for another 1–2 minutes. If the noodles begin to stick, add a splash of water. Stir in the parsley and serve sprinkled with the sesame seeds.

Hot-and-Sour Pork *or chicken*

This tasty dish is cooked in the oven and uses less oil than a stir-fry. Trim all visible fat from the pork before cooking, for a healthy, low-fat recipe.

INGREDIENTS

Serves 4

12 ounces pork fillet
1 teaspoon sunflower oil
1-inch piece fresh ginger, grated
1 fresh red chili, seeded and
  finely chopped
1 teaspoon Chinese five-spice powder
1 tablespoon sherry vinegar
1 tablespoon soy sauce
1 can (8 ounces) pineapple chunks in
  natural juice
¾ cup chicken broth
4 teaspoons cornstarch
1 tablespoon water
1 green bell pepper, seeded and sliced
4 ounces baby corn, halved
salt and freshly ground black pepper
sprig of flat-leaf parsley, to garnish
boiled rice, to serve

1 Trim away any visible fat from the pork and cut into ½-inch-thick slices using a sharp knife.

2 Brush the sunflower oil over the base of a flameproof casserole. Heat over medium heat, then fry the pork for about 2 minutes on each side, or until lightly browned.

3 Blend together the ginger, chili, Chinese five-spice powder, sherry vinegar and soy sauce.

4 Drain the pineapple chunks, reserving the juice. Make the broth up to 1¼ cups by adding the reserved juice, mix together with the spices and pour over the pork.

5 Slowly bring the chicken broth to a boil. Blend the cornstarch with the water and gradually stir into the pork. Add the green bell pepper and baby corn and season to taste.

6 Cover and cook in a preheated oven at 325°F for 30 minutes, or until the pork is tender. Stir in the pineapple and cook for another 5 minutes. Garnish with flat-leaf parsley and serve with boiled rice.

COOK'S TIP

Chinese five-spice powder is available from Asian food stores and some large supermarkets. However, if you cannot find it, you can create your own by combining equal quantities of cinnamon, cloves, Szechuan peppercorns, fennel seeds and ground star anise or anise seeds.

Chinese Sweet-and-Sour Pork

Sweet-and-sour pork must be one of the most popular dishes served in Chinese restaurants throughout the Western world. Unfortunately, it is often spoiled by cooks who use too much ketchup in the sauce. Here is a classic recipe from Canton, the city of its origin.

INGREDIENTS

Serves 4

12 ounces lean pork
¼ teaspoon salt
½ teaspoon ground Szechuan
  peppercorns
1 tablespoon Chinese rice wine or
  dry sherry
1 can (4 ounces) bamboo shoots
2 tablespoons all-purpose flour
1 egg, lightly beaten
vegetable oil, for deep-frying

For the sauce

1 tablespoon vegetable oil
1 garlic clove, finely chopped
1 scallion, cut into short sections
1 green bell pepper, seeded and diced
1 fresh red chili, seeded and cut into
  fine strips
1 tablespoon light soy sauce
2 tablespoons light brown sugar
2–3 tablespoons rice vinegar
1 tablespoon tomato paste
about ½ cup Basic Broth or water

1 Cut the pork into small bite-sized cubes and place in a shallow dish. Add the salt, peppercorns and rice wine or dry sherry and marinate for 15–20 minutes.

2 Drain the bamboo shoots and cut them into small cubes the same size as the pork.

3 Dust the pork with flour, dip in the beaten egg and coat with more flour. Heat the oil in a preheated wok and deep-fry the pork in moderately hot oil for 3–4 minutes, stirring to separate the pieces. Remove and drain.

4 Reheat the oil until hot, return the pork to the wok and add the bamboo shoots. Fry for about 1 minute, or until the pork is golden. Remove and drain well.

5 To make the sauce, heat the oil in a clean wok or frying pan and add the garlic, scallion, green bell pepper and red chili. Stir-fry for 30–40 seconds, then add the soy sauce, sugar, rice vinegar, tomato paste and broth or water. Bring to a boil, then add the pork and bamboo shoots. Heat through and stir to mix, then serve.

Pork and Vegetable Stir-fry

A quick and easy stir-fry of pork and a mixture of vegetables, this makes an excellent family lunch or supper dish.

INGREDIENTS

Serves 4
8 ounces can pineapple chunks
1 tablespoon cornstarch
2 tablespoons light soy sauce
1 tablespoon Chinese rice wine or
    dry sherry
1 tablespoon light brown sugar
1 tablespoon white wine vinegar
1 teaspoon Chinese five-spice powder
2 teaspoons olive oil
1 red onion, sliced
1 garlic clove, crushed
1 fresh red chili, seeded and chopped
1-inch piece fresh ginger
12 ounces lean pork tenderloin, cut
    into thin strips
3 medium carrots, cut into short thin
    sticks
1 red bell pepper, seeded and sliced
6 ounces snow peas, halved
4 ounces bean sprouts
1 can (7 ounces) corn kernels
2 tablespoons chopped fresh cilantro
salt
1 tablespoon toasted sesame seeds,
    to garnish

1 Drain the pineapple, reserving the juice. To make the sauce mixture: blend, in a small bowl, the cornstarch with the reserved pineapple juice. Add the soy sauce, rice wine or dry sherry, sugar, vinegar and five-spice powder, stir to mix and set aside.

2 Heat the oil in a preheated wok or large, nonstick frying pan. Add the onion, garlic, chili and ginger and stir-fry for 30 seconds. Add the pork and stir-fry for 2–3 minutes..

3 Add the carrots to the wok with the red bell pepper and stir-fry for 2–3 minutes. Add the snow peas, bean sprouts and corn and stir-fry for 1–2 minutes.

4 Pour in the sauce mixture and the reserved pineapple and stir-fry until the sauce thickens. Reduce the heat and stir-fry for another 1–2 minutes. Stir in the cilantro and season to taste. Sprinkle with sesame seeds and serve immediately.

Sweet-and-Sour Pork and Shrimp Soup

This main-course soup has a rich, sour flavor.

INGREDIENTS

Serves 4–6

8 ounces jumbo shrimp, raw or
　cooked, peeled
2 tablespoons tamarind sauce
juice of 2 limes
12 ounces lean pork, diced
1 small green guava, peeled, halved
　and seeded
1 small underripe mango, peeled,
　pitted and chopped
6¼ cups chicken broth
1 tablespoon fish sauce or soy sauce
10 ounces sweet potato, peeled and cut
　into even-sized pieces
8 ounces unripe tomatoes, quartered
4 ounces green beans, halved
1 star fruit, thickly sliced
3 ounces green cabbage, shredded
salt and freshly ground black pepper
lime wedges, to garnish

1 Devein the shrimp and set aside.
　Put the tamarind sauce and lime
juice in a saucepan.

2 Add the pork, guava and mango to
　the pan and pour in the broth. Add
the fish sauce or soy sauce, bring to a
boil, reduce the heat and simmer for
30 minutes.

3 Add the remaining fruit and
　vegetables and the shrimp and
simmer for another 10–15 minutes.
Season to taste. Transfer to a serving
dish and garnish with lime wedges.

Savory Pork Pies

This recipe from the Philippines
is a legacy of sixteenth-century
Spanish colonialism, with a
unique Eastern touch.

INGREDIENTS

Serves 6

1 tablespoon vegetable oil
1 medium onion, chopped
1 garlic clove, crushed
1 teaspoon chopped fresh thyme
4 ounces ground pork
1 teaspoon paprika
1 hard-cooked egg, chopped
1 medium gherkin, chopped
2 tablespoons chopped fresh parsley
12 ounces frozen pastry, thawed
salt and freshly ground black pepper
vegetable oil, for deep-frying

1 To make the filling, heat the oil in a
　saucepan, add the onions, garlic
and thyme and fry for 3–4 minutes.
Add the pork and paprika and stir-fry
until the meat is evenly browned.
Season and turn the mixture out into a
bowl. Set aside to cool. Add the hard-
cooked egg, gherkin and parsley.

2 Lightly knead the pastry on a
　floured surface, then roll out to a
15-inch square. Cut out 12 circles,
5 inches in diameter. Place 1
tablespoon of the filling on each circle,
moisten the edges with a little water,
fold over into a half-moon shape and
press the edges together to seal.

3 Heat the vegetable oil in a deep-
　fryer to 385°F. Deep-fry the pies,
3 at a time, for 1–2 minutes, or until
golden brown. Drain on paper towels
and keep warm while you fry the
remaining pies. Serve warm.

Lion's Head Casserole

The name of this dish—*shi zi tou* in Chinese—derives from the rather strange idea that the meatballs look like a lion's head and the Chinese cabbage resembles its mane.

INGREDIENTS

Serves 4–6
1 pound ground pork
2 teaspoons finely chopped scallion
1 teaspoon finely chopped fresh ginger
2 ounces mushrooms, chopped
2 ounces cooked jumbo shrimp, peeled, or crabmeat, finely chopped
1 tablespoon light soy sauce
1 teaspoon light brown sugar
1 tablespoon Chinese rice wine or dry sherry
1 tablespoon cornstarch
1½ pounds Chinese cabbage

3–4 tablespoons vegetable oil
1 teaspoon salt
1¼ cups Basic Broth or water

1 Combine the pork, scallion, ginger, mushrooms, shrimp or crabmeat, soy sauce, sugar, rice wine or dry sherry and cornstarch. Shape the mixture into 4–6 meatballs.

2 Cut the Chinese cabbage into large pieces, all about the same size.

3 Heat the oil in a preheated wok or large frying pan. Add the Chinese cabbage and salt and stir-fry for 2–3 minutes. Add the meatballs and the broth or water, bring to a boil, cover and simmer gently for 30–45 minutes. Serve immediately.

Stir-fried Pork with Vegetables

This dish is a perfect example of the Chinese way of balancing and harmonizing colours, flavors and textures.

INGREDIENTS

Serves 4
4 ounces firm tomatoes, skinned
6 ounces zucchini
1 scallion
8 ounces pork fillet, thinly sliced
1 tablespoon light soy sauce
1 teaspoon light brown sugar
1 teaspoon Chinese rice wine or dry sherry
2 teaspoons cornstarch paste
4 tablespoons vegetable oil
1 teaspoon salt (optional)
Basic Broth or water, if necessary

1 Cut the tomatoes and zucchini into wedges. Slice the scallion. Put the pork in a bowl with 1 teaspoon of the soy sauce, the sugar, rice wine or dry sherry and cornstarch paste. Set aside to marinate.

2 Heat the oil in a preheated wok and stir-fry the pork for 1 minute, or until it colors. Remove with a slotted spoon, set aside and keep warm.

3 Add the vegetables to the wok and stir-fry for 2 minutes. Add the salt, the pork and a little broth or water, if necessary, and stir-fry for 1 minute. Add the remaining soy sauce, mix well and serve.

POULTRY

The versatility of chicken has never been
so apparent—stir-fried with ginger,
baked with spices, braised in coconut
milk and even barbecued Thai-style—
and, of course, this chapter also includes
mouthwatering recipes for other types of
poultry. Some dishes are familiar
favorites, such as Chicken Teriyaki,
Duck and Ginger Chop Suey and
Peking Duck, while others offer new
and exciting combinations of ingredients.
Try Chili Duck with Crab and Cashew
Sauce, Green Curry Coconut Chicken
or Honey-glazed Quail with a Five-
Spice Marinade.

Chicken Curry with Rice Vermicelli

Lemon grass gives this South East Asian curry a wonderful lemony flavor and fragrance.

INGREDIENTS

Serves 4

1 chicken, about 3–3½ pounds
8 ounces sweet potatoes
4 tablespoons vegetable oil
1 onion, finely sliced
3 garlic cloves, crushed
2–3 tablespoons Thai curry powder
1 teaspoon sugar
2 teaspoons fish sauce
2½ cups coconut milk
1 lemon grass stalk, cut in half
12 ounces rice vermicelli, soaked in hot water until soft
1 lemon, cut into wedges, to serve

For the garnish

4 ounces bean sprouts
2 scallions, finely sliced diagonally
2 red chilies, seeded and finely sliced
8–10 mint leaves

1 Remove the skin from the chicken. Cut the flesh into small pieces, and set aside. Peel the sweet potatoes, and cut them into chunks, about the size of the chicken pieces.

2 Heat half the oil in a large saucepan. Add the onion and garlic, and fry until the onion softens.

3 Add the chicken pieces, and stir-fry until they change color. Stir in the curry powder. Season with salt and sugar, and mix thoroughly. Then stir in the fish sauce.

4 Pour in the coconut milk, and add the lemon grass. Cook over a low heat for 15 minutes.

5 Meanwhile, heat the remaining oil in a large frying pan. Fry the sweet potatoes until lightly golden. Using a slotted spoon, add them to the chicken. Cook for 10–15 minutes more, or until both the chicken and sweet potatoes are tender.

6 Drain the rice vermicelli, and cook it in a saucepan of boiling water for 3–5 minutes. Drain well. Place in shallow bowls with the chicken curry. Garnish with the bean sprouts, scallions, chilies and mint leaves, and serve with lemon wedges.

Gingered Chicken Noodles

A blend of ginger, spice and coconut milk flavors this delicious supper dish, which is made in minutes. For a real Asian touch, add a little fish sauce to taste, just before serving.

INGREDIENTS

Serves 4
12 ounces boneless chicken breasts, skinned
8 ounces zucchini
10 ounces eggplant
2 tablespoons vegetable oil
2-inch piece fresh ginger, chopped
6 scallions, sliced
2 teaspoons Thai green curry paste
1⅓ cups coconut milk
2 cups chicken broth
4 ounces medium egg noodles
3 tablespoons chopped fresh cilantro
1 tablespoon lemon juice
salt and freshly ground black pepper
chopped fresh cilantro, to garnish

1 Cut the chicken into bite-sized pieces. Halve the zucchini lengthwise and roughly chop them. Roughly chop the eggplant.

2 Heat the oil in a large saucepan and cook the chicken until golden. Remove with a slotted spoon and drain on paper towels.

3 Add a little more oil, if necessary, and cook the ginger and scallions for 3 minutes. Add the zucchini and cook for 2–3 minutes, or until they are beginning to turn golden. Stir in the Thai curry paste and cook for 1 minute.

4 Add the coconut milk, broth, eggplant and chicken and simmer for 10 minutes. Add the noodles and cook for another 5 minutes, or until the chicken is cooked and the noodles are tender. Stir in the cilantro and lemon juice and season to taste. Serve immediately garnished with chopped fresh cilantro.

Spicy Chicken Stir-fry

The chicken is marinated in an aromatic blend of spices and stir-fried with crisp vegetables. If you find it too spicy, serve with a spoonful of sour cream or yogurt. It's delicious hot or cold.

INGREDIENTS

Serves 4

½ teaspoon ground turmeric
½ teaspoon ground ginger
1 teaspoon salt
1 teaspoon freshly ground black pepper
2 teaspoons ground cumin
1 tablespoon ground coriander
1 tablespoon superfine sugar
1 pound skinless, boneless chicken breasts
1 bunch scallions
4 celery stalks
2 red bell peppers, seeded
1 yellow bell pepper, seeded
6 ounces zucchini
6 ounces snow peas or sugar snap peas
sunflower oil, for frying
1 tablespoon lime juice
1 tablespoon honey

1 Combine the turmeric, ginger, salt, pepper, cumin, coriander and sugar in a bowl and mix well.

2 Cut the chicken into bite-sized strips. Add to the spice mixture and stir to coat the chicken pieces thoroughly. Set aside.

3 Prepare the vegetables. Cut the scallions, celery and bell peppers into thin 2-inch-long strips. Cut the zucchini at a slight angle into thin rounds and trim the snow peas or sugar snap peas.

4 Heat 2 tablespoons of oil in a preheated wok or large frying pan. Stir-fry the chicken in batches until cooked through and golden brown, adding a little more oil if necessary. Remove from the pan and keep warm.

5 Add a little more oil to the pan and cook the scallions, celery, bell peppers and zucchini over medium heat for 8–10 minutes, or until beginning to soften and turn golden. Add the snow peas or sugar snap peas and cook for another 2 minutes.

6 Return the chicken to the pan, with the lime juice and honey. Cook for 2 minutes. Serve immediately.

Spicy Clay-Pot Chicken

Clay-pot cooking stems from the practice of burying a glazed pot in the embers of an open fire. The heat surrounds the base and keeps the liquid inside at a slow simmer, similar to the way a modern-day casserole works.

INGREDIENTS

Serves 4–6

3–3½ pounds chicken
3 tablespoons freshly shredded coconut
2 tablespoons vegetable oil
2 shallots or 1 small onion, finely chopped
2 garlic cloves, crushed
2-inch piece lemongrass
1-inch piece galangal or fresh ginger, thinly sliced
2 small fresh green chilies, seeded and finely chopped
½-inch square shrimp paste or 1 tablespoon fish sauce
1⅔ cups canned coconut milk
1¼ cups chicken broth
2 kaffir lime leaves (optional)
1 tablespoon sugar
1 tablespoon rice vinegar or white wine vinegar
2 ripe tomatoes, to garnish
2 tablespoons chopped cilantro leaves, to garnish

1 To separate the chicken, remove the legs and wings with a chopping knife. Skin the pieces, divide the drumsticks from the thighs and, using a pair of kitchen scissors, remove the lower part of the chicken, leaving the breast piece. Remove as many of the bones as you can, to make the dish easier to eat. Cut the breast piece into four pieces and set aside.

2 Dry-fry the coconut in a large wok until evenly brown. Add the vegetable oil, shallots or onion, garlic, lemongrass, galangal or ginger, chilies and shrimp paste or fish sauce. Fry briefly to release the flavors. Add the chicken pieces to the wok and brown evenly with the spices for 2–3 minutes.

3 Strain the coconut milk and reserve the thick part. Add the thin part to the wok, together with the chicken broth, lime leaves, if using, sugar and vinegar. Transfer to a ceramic casserole, cover and bake in a preheated oven at 350°F for 50–55 minutes, or until the chicken is tender. Stir in the thick part of the coconut milk and return to the oven for 5–10 minutes to simmer and thicken.

4 Place the tomatoes in a bowl and cover with boiling water to loosen and remove the skins. Halve the tomatoes, discard the seeds and cut into large dice. Add the tomatoes to the finished dish, scatter the chopped cilantro on top, and serve.

Green Curry Coconut Chicken

The recipe given here for green curry paste takes time to make properly. Pork, shrimp and fish can all be used instead of chicken, but cooking times must be adjusted accordingly.

INGREDIENTS

Serves 4–6

2½ pounds chicken
2½ cups coconut milk
1¾ cups chicken broth
2 kaffir lime leaves
12 ounces sweet potatoes, roughly
    chopped
12 ounces winter squash, seeded and
    roughly chopped
4 ounces green beans, halved
1 small bunch fresh cilantro, shredded,
    to garnish

For the green curry paste

2 teaspoons coriander seeds
½ teaspoon caraway or cumin seeds
3–4 medium fresh green chilies, finely
    chopped
4 teaspoons sugar
2 teaspoons salt
3-inch piece lemongrass
¼-inch piece galangal or fresh ginger,
    finely chopped
3 garlic cloves, crushed
4 shallots or 1 medium onion, finely
    chopped
¼-inch square shrimp paste
3 tablespoons finely chopped fresh
    cilantro
3 tablespoons finely chopped fresh mint
½ teaspoon ground nutmeg
2 tablespoons vegetable oil

1 To prepare the chicken, remove the legs, then separate the thighs from the drumsticks. Separate the lower part of the chicken carcass by cutting through the rib section with kitchen scissors. Divide the breast part in half down the middle, then chop each half in two. Remove the skin from all the pieces and discard.

2 Strain the coconut milk into a bowl, reserving the thick part. Place the chicken in a stainless steel or enamel saucepan and pour in the thin part of the coconut milk and the broth. Add the lime leaves and simmer, uncovered, for 40 minutes. Remove the chicken from the saucepan and allow to cool. Reserve the cooking liquid. Remove the cooled meat from the bone and set aside.

3 To make the curry paste, dry-fry the coriander seeds and caraway or cumin seeds in a large wok. Grind the chilies with the sugar and salt in a mortar with a pestle to make a smooth paste. Combine the seeds from the large wok with the chili paste, the lemongrass, galangal or ginger, garlic and shallots or onion, then grind until smooth. Add the shrimp paste, cilantro, mint, nutmeg and vegetable oil.

4 Place 1 cup of the reserved cooking liquid in a large wok. Add 4–5 tablespoons of the curry paste according to taste. Boil rapidly until the liquid has reduced completely. Add the remaining cooking liquid, chicken meat, sweet potatoes, squash and green beans. Simmer for 10–15 minutes, or until the potatoes are cooked. Stir in the thick part of the coconut milk and simmer gently to thicken. Serve garnished with cilantro.

Chicken Cooked in Coconut Milk

Traditionally, the chicken pieces would be part-cooked by frying, but roasting in the oven is a better option. *Ayam Opor* is an unusual recipe in that the sauce is white as it does not contain chilies or turmeric, unlike many other Indonesian dishes. The dish is usually served with crisp deep-fried onions.

INGREDIENTS

Serves 4

3–3½-pound chicken or
    4 chicken quarters
4 garlic cloves
1 onion, sliced
4 macadamia nuts or 8 almonds
1 tablespoon coriander seeds, dry-fried,
    or 1 teaspoon ground coriander
3 tablespoons oil
1 inch fresh *galangal*, peeled
    and bruised
2 lemon grass stems, fleshy part bruised
3 lime leaves
2 bay leaves
1 teaspoon sugar
2½ cups coconut milk
salt
boiled rice and deep-fried onions,
    to serve

1 Preheat the oven to 375°F. Cut the chicken into four or eight pieces. Season with salt. Put in an oiled roasting pan and cook in the oven for 25–30 minutes. Meanwhile, prepare the sauce.

2 Grind the garlic, onion, nuts and coriander to a fine paste in a food processor or with a mortar and pestle. Heat the oil and fry the paste to bring out the flavor. Do not allow it to brown.

3 Add the part-cooked chicken pieces to a wok together with the *laos*, lemon grass, lime and bay leaves, sugar, coconut milk and salt to taste. Mix well to coat in the sauce.

4 Bring to a boil and then reduce the heat and simmer gently for 30–40 minutes, uncovered, until the chicken is tender and the coconut sauce is reduced and thickened. Stir the mixture occasionally during cooking.

5 Just before serving remove the bruised *galangal* and lemongrass. Serve with boiled rice sprinkled with crisp deep-fried onions.

Chicken Teriyaki

A simple bowl of boiled rice is
the ideal accompaniment to this
subtle Japanese chicken dish.

INGREDIENTS

Serves 4

1 pound skinless, boneless chicken
breasts
orange segments and mustard and
watercress, to garnish

For the marinade

1 teaspoon sugar
1 tablespoon sake
1 tablespoon dry sherry
2 tablespoons dark soy sauce
grated rind of 1 orange

1 Slice the chicken into long, thin
strips using a cleaver or sharp knife.

2 To make the marinade, combine
all the marinade ingredients in
a bowl.

3 Place the chicken in a separate
bowl, pour the marinade over it
and marinate for 15 minutes.

4 Add the chicken and the marinade
to a preheated wok and stir-fry
for 4–5 minutes, or until it is cooked.
Serve garnished with orange segments
and mustard and watercress.

Shredded Chicken with Celery

The tender chicken breast contrasts with the crunchy texture of the celery, and the red chilies add color and flavor.

INGREDIENTS

Serves 4

10 ounces skinless, boneless chicken breasts
1 teaspoon salt
½ egg white, lightly beaten
2 teaspoons cornstarch paste
2 cups vegetable oil
1 celery heart, cut into fine strips
1–2 fresh red chilies, seeded and cut into fine strips
1 scallion, cut into fine strips
few strips of fresh ginger, cut into fine strips
1 teaspoon light brown sugar
1 tablespoon Chinese rice wine or dry sherry
few drops of sesame oil

1 Using a sharp knife, thinly shred the chicken. In a bowl, mix together a pinch of the salt, the egg white and the cornstarch paste. Stir in the chicken.

2 Heat the oil in a preheated wok, add the chicken and stir to separate the shreds. When the chicken turns white, remove with a strainer and drain. Keep warm.

3 Pour off all but 2 tablespoons of the oil. Add the celery, chilies, scallion and ginger to the wok and stir-fry for 1 minute. Add the chicken, remaining salt, sugar and rice wine or dry sherry. Cook for 1 minute, then add the sesame oil. Serve hot.

Chicken with Chinese Vegetables

This dish makes an excellent family main course served with rice or noodles, but can also be combined with a selection of other dishes to serve as part of a dinner party menu.

INGREDIENTS

Serves 4

8-10 ounces skinless, boneless chicken breasts
1 teaspoon salt
½ egg white, lightly beaten
2 teaspoons cornstarch paste
4 tablespoons vegetable oil
6–8 small dried shiitake mushrooms, soaked in hot water
4 ounces canned sliced bamboo shoots
4 ounces snow peas

1 scallion, cut into short sections
few small pieces of fresh ginger
1 teaspoon light brown sugar
1 tablespoon light soy sauce
1 tablespoon Chinese rice wine or dry sherry
few drops of sesame oil

1 Cut the chicken into thin slices, each about the size of an oblong postage stamp. Place in a bowl and mix with a pinch of the salt, the egg white and the cornstarch paste.

2 Heat the oil in a preheated wok, add the chicken and stir-fry over medium heat for about 30 seconds, then remove with a slotted spoon and keep warm.

3 Add the vegetables and ginger to the wok and stir-fry over high heat for about 1 minute. Add the remaining salt, sugar and chicken. Blend, then add the soy sauce and rice wine or dry sherry. Stir for another minute. Sprinkle with the sesame oil and serve.

Thai-style Chicken Livers

Chicken liver is a good source of iron and is a popular meat, especially in the north-east. Serve this dish as an appetizer with salad, or as part of a main course with jasmine rice.

INGREDIENTS

Serves 4–6
3 tablespoons vegetable oil
1 pound chicken livers, trimmed
4 shallots, chopped
2 garlic cloves, chopped
1 tablespoon roasted ground rice
3 tablespoons fish sauce
3 tablespoons lime juice
1 teaspoon sugar
2 lemongrass stalks, bruised
   and finely chopped
2 tablespoons chopped cilantro
10–12 mint leaves, to garnish

1 Heat the oil in a wok or large frying pan. Add the livers and fry over medium-high heat for about 4 minutes, until the liver is golden brown and cooked, but still pink inside.

2 Move the liver to one side of the pan and add the shallots and garlic. Fry for about 1–2 minutes.

3 Add the roasted ground rice, fish sauce, lime juice, sugar, lemongrass and cilantro. Stir to combine. Remove from the heat and serve garnished with mint leaves.

Barbecued Chicken

Barbecued chicken is served almost everywhere in Thailand, from roadside stalls to sports stadiums and beaches.

INGREDIENTS

Serves 4–6
1 chicken, about 3–3½ pounds, cut
   into 8–10 pieces
2 limes, cut into wedges and 2 red
   chilies, finely sliced, to garnish

For the marinade
2 lemongrass stalks, chopped
1-inch piece fresh ginger
6 garlic cloves
4 shallots
½ bunch cilantro roots
1 tablespoon palm sugar
½ cup unsweetened coconut milk
2 tablespoons fish sauce
2 tablespoons soy sauce

1 To make the marinade, put all the ingredients into a food processor and process until smooth.

2 Put the chicken pieces in a dish and pour over the marinade. Set aside in a cool place to marinate for at least 4 hours or overnight.

3 Barbecue the chicken over glowing coals, or place on a rack over a baking pan and bake at 400°F for about 20–30 minutes, or until the chicken is cooked and golden brown. Turn the pieces occasionally and brush them with the marinade.

4 Garnish with lime wedges and finely sliced red chilies.

Duck and Ginger Chop Suey

Chicken can also be used in this recipe, but duck gives a richer contrast of flavors.

INGREDIENTS

Serves 4

2 duck breasts, about 6 ounces each
3 tablespoons sunflower oil
1 small egg, lightly beaten
1 garlic clove
6 ounces bean sprouts
2 slices fresh ginger, cut into thin sticks
2 teaspoons oyster sauce
2 scallions, cut into thin sticks
salt and freshly ground black pepper

For the marinade

1 tablespoon honey
2 teaspoons Chinese rice wine or dry sherry
2 teaspoons light soy sauce
2 teaspoons dark soy sauce

1 Remove the fat and skin from the duck, cut the breasts into strips and place in a bowl. To make the marinade, combine all the marinade ingredients together, pour over the duck, cover, and marinate overnight in the refrigerator.

2 The next day, make the omelet. Heat a small frying pan and add 1 tablespoon of the oil. When the oil is hot, pour in the egg and swirl around to make an omelet. Once cooked, leave it to cool and then cut into strips. Drain the duck and discard the marinade.

3 Bruise the garlic with the flat side of a knife. Heat 2 teaspoons of the oil in a preheated wok. When the oil is hot, add the garlic and fry for 30 seconds, pressing it to release the flavor. Discard. Add the bean sprouts with seasoning and stir-fry for 30 seconds. Transfer to a heated dish, draining off any liquid.

4 Heat the remaining oil in a preheated wok. When the oil is hot, stir-fry the duck for 3 minutes, until cooked. Add the ginger and oyster sauce and stir-fry for another 2 minutes. Add the bean sprouts, egg strips and scallions, stir-fry briefly and serve.

Mandarin Sesame Duck

Duck is a high-fat meat, but it is possible to get rid of a considerable proportion of the fat by cooking it in this way. (If you remove the skin completely, the meat can be dry.) For a special occasion, duck breasts are an excellent choice, but they are more expensive than legs.

INGREDIENTS

Serves 4
4 duck legs or boneless breasts
2 tablespoons light soy sauce
3 tablespoons honey
1 tablespoon sesame seeds
4 mandarin oranges
1 teaspoon cornstarch
salt and freshly ground black pepper
mixed vegetables, to serve

1 Prick the duck skin all over. If using breasts, slash the skin diagonally at intervals with a small, sharp knife.

2 Place the duck on a rack in a roasting pan and roast for 1 hour in a preheated oven at 350°F. Combine 1 tablespoon of the soy sauce with 2 tablespoons of the honey and brush over the duck. Sprinkle with sesame seeds. Roast for 15–20 minutes, or until golden brown.

3 Meanwhile, grate the rind from one mandarin and squeeze the juice from that one plus one other. Combine the rind, juice and cornstarch, then stir in the remaining soy sauce and honey. Heat, stirring, until thickened and clear. Season to taste. Peel and slice the remaining mandarins. Serve the duck with the mandarin slices, sauce and mixed vegetables.

Peking Duck

This has to be the *pièce de résistance* of any Chinese banquet. It is not too difficult to prepare and cook at home—the secret is to use duckling with a low fat content. Also, make sure that the skin of the duck is absolutely dry before you start to cook—the drier the skin, the crispier the duck.

INGREDIENTS

Serves 6–8
5–5¼ pounds oven-ready duckling
2 tablespoons honey, dissolved in ⅔ cup warm water

For the duck sauce
2 tablespoons sesame oil
6–8 tablespoons yellow bean sauce, crushed
2–3 tablespoons light brown sugar

To serve
20–24 Thin Pancakes
6–8 scallions, thinly shredded
½ cucumber, thinly shredded

COOK'S TIP

If preferred, serve Peking Duck with plum sauce in place of the duck sauce. Plum sauce is available from Asian stores and larger supermarkets. Duck sauce can also be bought ready-made.

1 Remove any feather studs and any lumps of fat from inside the vent of the duck. Plunge the duck into a saucepan of boiling water for 2–3 minutes to seal the pores. This will make the skin airtight, thus preventing the fat from escaping during cooking. Remove the duck and drain well, then dry thoroughly.

2 Brush the duck all over with the dissolved honey, then hang the bird up in a cool place for at least 4–5 hours.

3 Place the duck, breast side up, on a rack in a roasting pan and cook in a preheated oven at 400°F for 1½–1¾ hours without either basting or turning.

4 Meanwhile, make the duck sauce. Heat the sesame oil in a small saucepan. Add the crushed yellow bean sauce and the light brown sugar. Stir until smooth and allow to cool.

5 To serve, peel off the crispy duck skin in small slices using a sharp carving knife or cleaver, then carve the juicy meat in thin strips. Arrange the skin and meat on separate serving plates.

6 Open a pancake on each plate and spread about 1 teaspoon of the chosen sauce in the middle, with a few strips of shredded scallion and cucumber. Top with 2–3 slices each of duck skin and meat. Roll up and eat.

Crispy and Aromatic Duck

Because this dish is often served with pancakes, scallions, cucumber and duck sauce, many people mistakenly think this is Peking Duck. This recipe, however, uses quite a different cooking method. The result is just as crispy but the delightful aroma makes this dish particularly distinctive. Plum sauce may be substituted for the duck sauce.

INGREDIENTS

Serves 6–8

4–4¼ pounds oven ready duckling
2 teaspoons salt
5–6 whole star anise
1 tablespoon Szechuan peppercorns
1 teaspoon cloves
2–3 cinnamon sticks
3–4 scallions
3–4 slices fresh ginger, unpeeled
5–6 tablespoons Chinese rice wine or dry sherry
vegetable oil, for deep-frying

To serve

lettuce leaves
20–24 Thin Pancakes
½ cup duck sauce
6–8 scallions, cut into fine strips
½ cucumber, cut into fine strips

1 Remove the wings from the duck. Split the body in half down the length of the backbone.

2 Rub salt all over the two duck halves, taking care to rub it in well.

3 Place the duck in a dish with the star anise, peppercorns, cloves, cinnamon, scallions, ginger and rice wine or dry sherry and marinate for at least 4–6 hours.

4 Place the duck with the marinade in a steamer positioned in a wok partly filled with boiling water and steam vigorously for 3–4 hours (longer if possible). Remove the duck from the cooking liquid and let cool for at least 5–6 hours. The duck must be completely cool and dry or the skin will not become crispy.

5 Heat the oil in a preheated wok until smoking, place the duck pieces in the oil, skin side down, and deep-fry for 5–6 minutes, or until crisp and brown, turning just once at the very last moment.

6 Remove, drain, take the meat off the bone and place on a bed of lettuce leaves. To serve, wrap a portion of duck in each pancake with a little sauce, scallions and cucumber. Eat with your fingers.

Chili Duck with Crab and Cashew Sauce

This spicy dish would be delicious served with Thai rice, which is slightly aromatic.

INGREDIENTS

Serves 4–6

6 pounds duck
5 cups water
2 kaffir lime leaves
1½ teaspoons salt
2–3 small fresh red chilies, seeded and finely chopped
5 teaspoons sugar
2 tablespoons coriander seeds
1 teaspoon caraway seeds
1 cup raw cashews, chopped
3-inch piece lemongrass
1 inch piece galangal or fresh ginger, finely chopped
2 garlic cloves, crushed
4 shallots or 1 medium onion, finely chopped
¾-inch square shrimp paste
1 ounce cilantro white root or stem, finely chopped
6 ounces frozen white crabmeat, thawed
2 ounces creamed coconut
1 small bunch fresh cilantro, chopped, to garnish
boiled rice, to serve

1 Remove the legs from the duck, separate the thighs from the drumsticks and chop each thigh and drumstick into two pieces. Trim away the lower half of the duck with kitchen scissors. Cut the breast piece in half down the middle, then chop each half into four pieces.

2 Put the duck flesh and bones in a large saucepan and cover with the water. Add the lime leaves and 1 teaspoon of the salt, bring to a boil and simmer for 30–45 minutes, or until the meat is tender. Discard the duck bones. Skim off the fat from the broth and set the broth aside.

3 Grind together the chilies, sugar and remaining salt in a mortar with a pestle or in a food processor. Dry-fry the coriander seeds, caraway seeds and cashews in a preheated wok for 1–2 minutes to release their flavor. Add the seeds and nuts to the chili mixture, together with the lemongrass, galangal or ginger, garlic and shallots or onion and reduce to a smooth paste. Add the shrimp paste and cilantro root or stem and mix well.

4 Add 1 cup of the reserved broth and blend to make a thin paste.

5 Pour the spice mixture into the saucepan with the duck and mix thoroughly. Bring to a boil, lower the heat and simmer for 20–25 minutes.

6 Add the crabmeat and creamed coconut and simmer briefly to heat through. Turn out onto a warmed serving dish, garnish with the chopped cilantro and accompany with boiled rice.

Stir-fried Turkey with Snow Peas

Turkey is often a rather disappointing meat with a bland flavor. Here it is enlivened with a delicious marinade and combined with crunchy nuts to provide contrasting textures.

INGREDIENTS

Serves 4

2 tablespoons sesame oil
6 tablespoons lemon juice
1 garlic clove, crushed
½-inch piece fresh ginger, grated
1 teaspoon honey
1 pound turkey fillets, skinned and cut
 into strips
4 ounces snow peas
2 tablespoons peanut oil
2 ounces cashews
6 scallions, cut into strips
1 can (8 ounces) water chestnuts,
 drained and thinly sliced
salt
saffron rice, to serve

3 Drain the marinade from the turkey strips and reserve the marinade. Heat the peanut oil in a preheated wok or large frying pan, add the cashews and stir-fry for 1–2 minutes, or until golden brown. Remove the cashews from the wok or frying pan using a slotted spoon, and set aside.

4 Add the turkey to the wok or frying pan and stir-fry for 3–4 minutes, or until golden brown. Add the scallions, snow peas, water chestnuts and reserved marinade. Cook for a few minutes, until the turkey is tender and the sauce is bubbling and hot. Stir in the cashews and serve with saffron rice.

1 Combine the sesame oil, lemon juice, garlic, ginger and honey in a shallow, nonmetallic dish. Add the turkey and mix well. Cover and marinate for 3–4 hours.

2 Blanch the snow peas in boiling salted water for 1 minute. Drain, refresh under cold running water and set aside.

Honey-glazed Quail with a Five-Spice Marinade

Although the quail is a relatively small bird—four to five ounces—it is surprisingly meaty. One bird is usually sufficient for one serving.

INGREDIENTS

Serves 4
4 oven-ready quail
2 pieces star anise
2 teaspoons ground cinnamon
2 teaspoons fennel seeds
2 teaspoons ground Szechuan or
    Chinese pepper
pinch of ground cloves
1 small onion, finely chopped
1 garlic clove, crushed
4 tablespoons honey
2 tablespoons dark soy sauce
2 scallions, roughly chopped, finely
    grated rind of 1 mandarin orange or
    satsuma and radish and carrot
    "flowers," to garnish
banana leaves, to serve

1 Remove the backbones from the quail by cutting down either side with a pair of kitchen scissors.

2 Flatten the birds with the palm of your hand and secure each one with two bamboo skewers.

3 Grind together the star anise, cinnamon, fennel seeds, pepper and cloves in a mortar with a pestle. Add the onion, garlic, honey and soy sauce and mix well.

4 Place the quail on a flat dish, cover with the spice mixture and marinate for at least 8 hours.

5 Cook the quail under a preheated broiler or on a grill for 7–8 minutes on each side, basting from time to time with the marinade.

6 Arrange the quail on a bed of banana leaves and garnish with the scallions, orange or satsuma rind and radish and carrot "flowers."

VEGETABLES

Unusual ways of preparing familiar vegetables, as well as dishes using more exotic ingredients, can spice up Western grills and roasts or form part of an all Asian meal. Stir-frying is an especially good way of cooking vegetables without losing flavor, texture, color and valuable nutrients. There are recipes for all tastes: palate-tingling Bok Choy with Lime Dressing, Chinese Vegetable Stir-fry with its colorful, crunchy mix of ingredients, Chinese Garlic Mushrooms, the perfect vegetarian snack, and even Chinese-style Brussels sprouts!

Daikon, Beet and Carrot Stir-fry

This is a dazzlingly colorful dish with a crunchy texture and fragrant taste.

INGREDIENTS

Serves 4

¼ cup pine nuts
4 ounces daikon, peeled
4 ounces raw beet, peeled
2 medium carrots, peeled
1½ tablespoons vegetable oil
juice of 1 orange
2 tablespoons chopped fresh cilantro
salt and freshly ground black pepper

1 Place the pine nuts in a preheated wok and toss until golden brown. Remove and set aside.

2 Cut the daikon, beet and carrots into long, thin strips.

3 Heat the oil in a preheated wok. When the oil is hot, stir-fry the daikon, beet and carrots for 2–3 minutes. Remove and set aside.

4 Pour the orange juice into the wok and simmer for 2 minutes. Remove and keep warm.

5 Arrange the vegetables attractively on a warmed platter, sprinkle the cilantro on top, and season to taste with salt and pepper.

6 Drizzle with the orange juice, sprinkle with the pine nuts, and serve immediately.

Bok Choy with Lime Dressing

For this Thai recipe, the coconut dressing is traditionally made using fish sauce, but vegetarians could use mushroom sauce instead. Beware, the red chilies make this a fiery dish!

INGREDIENTS

Serves 4
6 scallions
2 bok choy
2 tablespoons oil
3 fresh red chilies, cut into thin strips
4 garlic cloves, thinly sliced
1 tablespoon crushed peanuts

For the dressing
1–2 tablespoons fish sauce
2 tablespoons lime juice
1 cup coconut milk

1 To make the dressing, blend together the fish sauce and lime juice, then stir in the coconut milk.

2 Trim the scallions, then cut diagonally into slices, including all but the very tips of the green parts, but keeping the green and white parts separate.

3 Using a large, sharp knife, cut the bok choy into very fine strips.

4 Heat the oil in a preheated wok and stir-fry the chilies for 2–3 minutes, or until crisp. Transfer to a plate using a slotted spoon. Stir-fry the garlic for 30–60 seconds, or until golden brown, and transfer to the plate with the chilies. Stir-fry the white parts of the scallions for about 2–3 minutes and then add the green parts and stir-fry for another minute. Add to the plate with the chilies and garlic.

5 Bring a large pan of salted water to a boil and add the bok choy. Stir twice and then drain immediately. Place the warmed bok choy in a large bowl, add the coconut dressing and stir well. Spoon into a large serving bowl and sprinkle with the crushed peanuts and the stir-fried chili mixture. Serve immediately.

Stir-fried Vegetables with Pasta

This colorful Chinese-style dish is easily prepared and, for a change, uses pasta instead of Chinese noodles.

INGREDIENTS

Serves 4

1 medium carrot
6 ounces small zucchini
6 ounces green beans
6 ounces baby corn
1 pound ribbon pasta, such as tagliatelle
2 tablespoons corn oil, plus extra for
  tossing the pasta
½-inch piece fresh ginger, finely
  chopped
2 garlic cloves, finely chopped
6 tablespoons yellow bean sauce
6 scallions, sliced into 1-inch lengths
2 tablespoons dry sherry
1 teaspoon toasted sesame seeds
salt

1 Slice the carrot and zucchini diagonally into chunks. Slice the green beans diagonally. Cut the baby corn diagonally in half.

2 Cook the pasta in plenty of boiling salted water according to the package instructions, drain, then rinse under hot water. Toss with a little oil to prevent sticking. Set aside.

3 Heat the 2 tablespoons of oil in a preheated wok or frying pan and add the ginger and garlic. Stir-fry for 30 seconds, then add the carrots, green beans, baby corn and zucchini.

4 Stir-fry for 3–4 minutes, then stir in the yellow bean sauce. Stir-fry for 2 minutes, add the scallions, dry sherry and pasta and stir-fry for another minute, until piping hot. Sprinkle with sesame seeds and serve immediately.

Chinese Vegetable Stir-fry

This is a typical stir-fried vegetable dish popular all over China. Chinese cabbage is like a cross between a cabbage and a crunchy lettuce, with a delicious peppery flavor.

INGREDIENTS

Serves 4

3 tablespoons sunflower oil
1 tablespoon sesame oil
1 garlic clove, chopped
8 ounces broccoli florets, cut into small
  pieces
4 ounces sugar snap peas
1 head Chinese cabbage, about
  1 pound, or Savoy cabbage, sliced
4 scallions, finely chopped
2 tablespoons soy sauce
2 tablespoons Chinese rice wine or
  dry sherry
2–3 tablespoons water
1 tablespoon sesame seeds, lightly
  toasted

1 Heat the sunflower and sesame oils in a preheated wok or large frying pan, add the garlic and stir-fry for 30 seconds.

2 Add the broccoli florets and stir-fry for 3 minutes. Add the sugar snap peas and cook for 2 minutes, then toss in the Chinese or Savoy cabbage and the scallions and stir-fry for another 2 minutes.

3 Pour in the soy sauce, rice wine or dry sherry and water and stir-fry for another 4 minutes, or until the vegetables are just tender. Sprinkle with the toasted sesame seeds and serve hot.

Indonesian Potatoes with Onions and Chili Sauce

This adds another dimension to French fries, with the addition of crisply fried onions and a spicy soy sauce and chili dressing. Eat *Kentang Gula* hot, warm or cold, as a tasty snack.

INGREDIENTS

Serves 6
3 large potatoes, about 8 ounces each, peeled and cut for fries
sunflower or peanut oil for deep-frying
2 onions, finely sliced
salt

For the dressing
1–2 fresh red chilies, seeded and ground
3 tablespoons dark soy sauce

1 Rinse the potatoes and then thoroughly pat dry with paper towels. Heat the oil and deep-fry the potatoes, until they are golden brown in color and crisp.

2 Put the potatoes in a dish, sprinkle with salt and keep warm. Fry the onion slices in the hot oil until they are similarly crisp and golden brown. Drain well on paper towels and then add to the potatoes.

3 Combine the chilies with the soy sauce and heat gently.

4 Pour over the potato and onion mixture and serve as suggested.

VARIATION

Alternatively, boil the potatoes in their skins. Drain, cool, peel and slice them, then shallow-fry until golden. Cook the onions and pour over the dressing.

Zucchini with Noodles

Any zucchini or member of the squash family can be used in *Oseng Oseng*, which is reminiscent of a similar dish eaten in Malaysia, whose cuisine has strong links with Indonesia.

INGREDIENTS

Serves 4–6
1 pound zucchini, sliced
1 onion, finely sliced
1 garlic clove, finely chopped
2 tablespoons sunflower oil
½ teaspoon ground turmeric
2 tomatoes, chopped
3 tablespoons water
14 ounces cooked, peeled shrimp (optional)
1 ounce cellophane noodles
salt

1 Use a vegetable peeler to cut thin strips from the outside of each zucchini. Cut the strips in neat slices. Set the zucchini on one side. Fry the onion and garlic in hot oil; do not allow to brown.

2 Add the turmeric, zucchini slices, chopped tomatoes, water and shrimp, if using.

3 Put the noodles in a pan and pour over boiling water to cover, let stand for a minute and then drain. Cut the noodles in 2-inch lengths and add to the vegetables.

4 Cover with a lid and cook in their own steam for 2–3 minutes. Toss everything well together. Season with salt to taste and serve while still hot.

Eggplant with Sesame Chicken

Young vegetables are prized in Japan for their sweet, delicate flavor. Here, small eggplants are stuffed with seasoned chicken.

Ingredients

Serves 4

6 ounces chicken breast or thighs, skinned
1 scallion, green part only, finely chopped
1 tablespoon dark soy sauce
1 tablespoon mirin or sweet sherry
½ teaspoon sesame oil
½ teaspoon salt
4 small eggplants, about 4 inches long
1 tablespoon sesame seeds
flour, for dusting
vegetable oil, for deep-frying

For the dipping sauce
4 tablespoons dark soy sauce
4 tablespoons dashi or vegetable broth
3 tablespoons mirin or sweet sherry

3 To make the dipping sauce, combine the soy sauce, dashi or broth and mirin or sherry. Pour into a shallow bowl and set aside.

4 Heat the vegetable oil in a wok or deep-fryer to 385°F. Fry the eggplants, two at a time, for 3–4 minutes. Lift out with chopsticks or a slotted spoon and drain on paper towels. Serve with the dipping sauce.

1 Remove the chicken meat from the bone and grind it finely in a food processor for 1–2 minutes. Add the scallion, soy sauce, mirin or sherry, sesame oil and salt.

2 Make four slits in each eggplant, so they remain joined at the stem. Spoon the ground chicken mixture into the eggplants, opening them slightly to accommodate it. Dip the fat end of each stuffed eggplant in the sesame seeds, then dust with flour. Set aside.

Chinese Potatoes with Chili Beans

East meets West. An American-style dish with a Chinese flavor—the sauce is particularly tasty. Try it as a supper dish when you're in the mood for a meal with a zing!

INGREDIENTS

Serves 4

4 medium potatoes, cut into thick chunks
2 tablespoons sunflower or peanut oil
3 scallions, sliced
1 large fresh red chili, seeded and sliced
2 garlic cloves, crushed
1 can (14 ounces) red kidney beans, drained
2 tablespoons soy sauce
1 tablespoon sesame oil
salt and freshly ground black pepper
1 tablespoon sesame seeds and chopped fresh cilantro or parsley, to garnish

1 Boil the potatoes until they are just tender. Take care not to overcook them. Drain and set aside.

2 Heat the sunflower or peanut oil in a preheated wok or large frying pan, stir-fry the scallions and chili for about 1 minute, then add the garlic and fry for a few seconds longer.

3 Add the potatoes, stirring well, then the beans and finally the soy sauce and sesame oil.

4 Season to taste and cook the vegetables until they are heated through. Sprinkle with sesame seeds and cilantro or parsley and serve.

Chinese Garlic Mushrooms

Tofu is high in protein and very low in fat, so it is an extremely useful and healthful food to keep handy for quick meals and snacks like this one.

INGREDIENTS

Serves 4

8 large, open mushrooms
3 scallions, sliced
1 garlic clove, crushed
2 tablespoons oyster sauce
10 ounces marinated firm tofu, cut into small dice
1 can (7 ounces) corn kernels, drained
2 teaspoons sesame oil
salt and freshly ground black pepper
1 scallion, cut into thin stips, to garnish

1 Finely chop the mushroom stalks and mix with the scallions, garlic and oyster sauce.

2 Stir in the diced, marinated tofu and the corn, season well with salt and pepper, then spoon the filling into the mushrooms.

3 Brush the edges of the mushrooms with the sesame oil. Arrange the stuffed mushrooms in a baking dish and bake in a preheated oven at 400°F for 12–15 minutes, or until the mushrooms are just tender, then serve at once, garnished with the scallion strips.

COOK'S TIP

If you prefer, omit the oyster sauce and use light soy sauce instead.

Stir-fried Mixed Vegetables

When selecting different items for a stir-fried dish, never mix the ingredients indiscriminately. The idea is to achieve a harmonious balance of color and texture.

INGREDIENTS

Serves 4
8 ounces Chinese cabbage
4 ounces baby corn
4 ounces broccoli
1 medium carrot
4 tablespoons vegetable oil
1 teaspoon salt
1 teaspoon light brown sugar
Basic Broth or water, if necessary
1 tablespoon light soy sauce
few drops of sesame oil (optional)

2 Heat the oil in a preheated wok and stir-fry the vegetables for about 2 minutes.

3 Add the salt and sugar and a little broth or water, if necessary, and continue stirring for another minute. Add the soy sauce and sesame oil, if using. Blend well and serve.

1 Cut the vegetables into roughly similar shapes and sizes.

Chinese Cabbage and Daikon with Scallops

A speedy stir-fry made using Chinese cabbage, daikon and scallops. Both the Chinese cabbage and daikon have a pleasant crunchy "bite." You need to work quickly, so have everything prepared before you start cooking.

INGREDIENTS

Serves 4

10 large scallops
5 tablespoons vegetable oil
3 garlic cloves, finely chopped
½-inch piece fresh ginger, finely sliced
4–5 scallions, cut lengthwise into
   1-inch pieces
2 tablespoons Chinese rice wine or
   dry sherry
½ daikon, cut into ½-inch slices
1 Chinese cabbage, chopped lengthwise
   into thin strips
4 tablespoons water

For the marinade
1 teaspoon cornstarch
1 egg white, lightly beaten
pinch of white pepper

For the sauce
1 teaspoon cornstarch
4 tablespoons water
3 tablespoons oyster sauce

1 Rinse the scallops and separate the roes from the white meat. Cut each scallop into two pieces and slice the roes. Place them on two separate dishes. For the marinade, blend together the cornstarch, egg white and white pepper. Pour over the scallops. Set aside for 10 minutes.

2 To make the sauce, blend the cornstarch with the water and the oyster sauce and set aside.

3 Heat about 2 tablespoons of the oil in a preheated wok, add half the garlic and let it sizzle, then add half the ginger and half the scallions. Stir-fry for about 30 seconds, then stir in the scallops. Stir-fry for up to 1 minute, or until the scallops start to become opaque. Reduce the heat and add 1 tablespoon of the rice wine or dry sherry. Cook briefly, then spoon the scallops and the cooking liquid into a bowl and set aside.

4 Heat another 2 tablespoons of the oil in the wok, add the remaining garlic, ginger and scallions and stir-fry for 1 minute. Add the roes and the remaining rice wine or dry sherry, stir-fry briefly and transfer to a dish.

5 Heat the remaining oil and add the daikon. Stir-fry for about 30 seconds, then stir in the cabbage. Stir-fry for about 30 seconds and add the oyster sauce mixture and the water. Allow the cabbage to simmer briefly. Stir in the scallops and cooking liquid. Cook briefly to heat through.

Tofu and Green Bean Red Curry

This is another curry that is simple and quick to make. This recipe uses green beans, but you can use almost any kind of vegetable, such as eggplant, bamboo shoots or broccoli.

INGREDIENTS

Serves 4–6
2½ cups unsweetened coconut milk
1 tablespoon red curry paste
3 tablespoons fish sauce
2 teaspoons palm sugar
3½ cups button mushrooms
4 ounces green beans, trimmed
6 ounces tofu, rinsed and cut into
   ¾-inch cubes
4 kaffir lime leaves, torn
2 red chilies, sliced
cilantro leaves, to garnish

1 Put about one-third of the coconut milk in a wok or saucepan. Cook until it starts to separate and an oily sheen appears.

2 Add the red curry paste, fish sauce and sugar to the coconut milk. Mix together thoroughly.

3 Add the mushrooms. Stir and cook for 1 minute.

4 Stir in the rest of the coconut milk and bring back to a boil.

5 Add the green beans and cubes of tofu and simmer gently for another 4–5 minutes.

6 Stir in the kaffir lime leaves and chilies. Serve garnished with the cilantro leaves.

Spiced Tofu Stir-fry

You could add any quickly cooked vegetable to this stir-fry—try snow peas, sugar snap peas, leeks or thin slices of carrot.

INGREDIENTS

Serves 4

2 teaspoons ground cumin
1 tablespoon paprika
1 teaspoon ground ginger
generous pinch of cayenne pepper
1 tablespoon superfine sugar
10 ounces firm tofu
oil, for frying
2 garlic cloves, crushed
1 bunch scallions, sliced
1 red bell pepper, seeded and sliced
1 yellow bell pepper, seeded and sliced
8 ounces button mushrooms, halved, or
    quartered if very large
1 large zucchini, sliced
4 ounces green beans, halved
½ cup pine nuts
1 tablespoon lime juice
1 tablespoon honey
salt and freshly ground black pepper

3 Add a little more oil to the wok or frying pan and stir-fry the garlic and scallions for 3 minutes. Add the remaining vegetables and stir-fry over medium heat for 6 minutes, or until they are beginning to soften and turn golden. Season well.

4 Return the tofu to the pan with the pine nuts, lime juice and honey. Heat through and serve.

1 Combine the cumin, paprika, ginger, cayenne and sugar with plenty of seasoning. Cut the tofu into cubes and coat them thoroughly in the spice mixture.

2 Heat some oil in a preheated wok or large frying pan. Cook the tofu over high heat for 3–4 minutes, turning occasionally. Take care not to break up the tofu too much. Remove with a slotted spoon. Wipe out the wok or pan with paper towels.

Chinese Sprouts

If you are bored with plain boiled Brussels sprouts, try pepping them up with this unusual stir-fried method, which uses a minimum of oil.

INGREDIENTS

Serves 4
1 pound Brussels sprouts
1 teaspoon sesame or sunflower oil
2 scallions, sliced
½ teaspoon Chinese five-spice powder
1 tablespoon light soy sauce

1 Trim the Brussels sprouts, then shred them finely using a large sharp knife. Alternatively, shred them in a food processor.

2 Heat the oil in a preheated wok or frying pan and add the sprouts and scallions, then stir-fry for 2 minutes, without browning.

3 Stir in the five-spice powder and soy sauce, then cook, stirring, for another 2–3 minutes, or until just tender.

4 Serve hot, with grilled meat or fish or with Chinese dishes.

COOK'S TIP

Brussels sprouts are rich in vitamin C, and this is a good way to cook them to preserve the nutrients. Larger sprouts cook particularly well by this method; and cabbage can be cooked in the same way.

SALADS

*There is much more to Asian salads
than a few leaves of Chinese cabbage
and a bunch of bean sprouts. The superb
collection of recipes here includes
flamboyant combinations of raw fruit
and vegetables, surprisingly refreshing
warm salads, startling pairings of sweet
and spicy ingredients, dramatic mixtures
of crunchy and melt-in-the mouth
textures and daring matching of flavors.
Try Thai Fruit and Vegetable Salad,
Warm Stir-fried Salad, Hot Coconut
Shrimp and Papaya Salad, Sesame
Noodle Salad with Hot Peanuts or
Duck, Avocado and Raspberry Salad.*

Chinese-style Chicken Salad

This delicious salad is a masterpiece of subtle flavors and contrasts in texture.

INGREDIENTS

Serves 4

4 boneless chicken breasts, about
    6 ounces each
4 tablespoons dark soy sauce
pinch of Chinese five-spice powder
generous squeeze of lemon juice
½ cucumber, peeled and cut into short
    thin sticks
1 teaspoon salt
3 tablespoons sunflower oil
2 tablespoons sesame oil
1 tablespoon sesame seeds
2 tablespoons Chinese rice wine or
    dry sherry
2 medium carrots, cut into short thin
    sticks
8 scallions, cut into fine strips
3 ounces bean sprouts

For the sauce
4 tablespoons crunchy peanut butter
2 teaspoons lemon juice
2 teaspoons sesame oil
¼ teaspoon hot chili powder
1 scallion, finely chopped

1 Put the chicken portions in a large pan and add just enough water to cover. Add 1 tablespoon of the soy sauce, the Chinese five-spice powder and the lemon juice, cover and bring to a boil, then simmer for about 20 minutes.

2 Meanwhile, place the cucumber sticks in a colander, sprinkle with the salt and cover with a plate with a weight on top. Let drain for 30 minutes—set the colander in a bowl to catch the liquid.

3 Lift out the poached chicken with a slotted spoon and let sit until cool enough to handle. Remove and discard the skin. Pound the chicken lightly with a rolling pin to loosen the fibers. Slice into thin strips and set aside.

4 Heat the sunflower and sesame oils in a preheated wok. Add the sesame seeds, fry for 30 seconds and then stir in the remaining soy sauce and the rice wine or dry sherry.

5 Add the carrots and stir-fry for 2–3 minutes, or until just tender. Remove from the heat and set aside.

6 Rinse the cucumber well, pat dry with paper towels and place in a bowl. Add the scallions, bean sprouts, cooked carrots, pan juices and shredded chicken and mix together. Transfer to a shallow dish. Cover and chill for about 1 hour, turning the mixture in the juices once or twice.

7 To make the sauce, cream the peanut butter with the lemon juice, sesame oil and chili powder, adding a little hot water to form a paste, then stir in the scallion. Arrange the chicken mixture on a serving dish and serve with the peanut sauce.

Shrimp Noodle Salad with Fragrant Herbs

A light, refreshing salad with all the tangy flavor of the sea. Instead of shrimp, try squid, scallops, mussels or crab.

INGREDIENTS

Serves 4

4 ounces cellophane noodles, soaked in
   hot water until soft
16 cooked shrimp, peeled
1 small green bell pepper, seeded and
   cut into strips
½ cucumber, cut into strips
1 tomato, cut into strips
2 shallots, finely sliced
salt and freshly ground black pepper
cilantro leaves, to garnish

For the dressing

1 tablespoon rice vinegar
2 tablespoons fish sauce
2 tablespoons fresh lime juice
pinch of salt
½ teaspoon grated fresh ginger
1 lemon grass stalk, finely chopped
1 red chili, seeded and finely sliced
2 tablespoons coarsely chopped mint
few sprigs tarragon, coarsely chopped
1 tablespoon snipped chives

1 Make the dressing by combining all the ingredients in a small bowl or cup. Whisk well.

2 Drain the noodles, then plunge them in a saucepan of boiling water for 1 minute. Drain, rinse under cold running water, and drain again well.

3 In a large bowl, combine the noodles with the shrimp, pepper, cucumber, tomato and shallots. Lightly season with salt and pepper, then toss with the dressing.

4 Spoon the noodles onto individual plates, arranging the shrimp on top. Garnish with a few cilantro leaves, and serve at once.

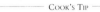

--- COOK'S TIP ---

Shrimp are available pre-cooked and often shelled. To cook shrimp, boil them for 5 minutes. Allow them to cool in the cooking liquid, then gently pull off the tail shell and twist off the head.

Warm Stir-fried Salad

Warm salads are becoming increasingly popular, because they are both delicious and nutritious. Arrange the salad greens on four individual plates so the hot stir-fry can quickly be served on them, ensuring that the greens remain crisp and the chicken warm.

INGREDIENTS

Serves 4

few large sprigs of fresh tarragon
2 skinless, boneless chicken breasts, about 8 ounces each
2-inch piece ginger, peeled and finely chopped
3 tablespoons light soy sauce
1 tablespoon sugar
1 tablespoon sunflower oil
1 Chinese lettuce
½ frisée head of lettuce, torn into bite-sized pieces
1 cup unsalted cashews
2 large carrots, cut into fine strips
salt and freshly ground black pepper

1 Strip the tarragon leaves from the stems and chop the leaves.

2 Cut the chicken into fine strips and place in a bowl.

3 To make the marinade, mix together in a bowl the tarragon, ginger, soy sauce, sugar and seasoning.

4 Pour the marinade over the chicken strips and marinate for 2–4 hours in a cool place.

5 Strain the chicken and reserve the marinade. Heat the oil in a preheated wok. When the oil is hot, stir-fry the chicken for 3 minutes, then add the marinade and allow to bubble for 2–3 minutes.

6 Slice the Chinese lettuce and arrange on a plate with the frisée. Toss the cashews and carrots together with the chicken, pile on top of the bed of lettuce and serve immediately.

Thai Beef Salad

A hearty salad of beef, laced with a chili and lime dressing.

INGREDIENTS

Serves 4

2 x 8-ounce sirloin steaks
1 red onion, finely sliced
½ cucumber, finely sliced into matchsticks
1 lemongrass stalk, finely chopped
juice of 2 limes
1–2 tablespoons fish sauce
2 tablespoons chopped scallions
2–4 red chilies, finely sliced, to garnish
fresh cilantro, Chinese mustard cress and mint leaves, to garnish

1 Pan-fry or broil the beef steaks to medium-rare. Allow to rest for 10–15 minutes.

2 When cool, thinly slice the beef and put the slices in a large bowl.

3 Add the sliced onion, cucumber matchsticks and lemongrass.

4 Add the scallions. Toss and season with lime juice and fish sauce. Serve at room temperature or chilled, garnished with the chilies, cilantro, Chinese mustard cress and mint.

Tangy Chicken Salad

This fresh and lively dish typifies the character of Thai cuisine. It is ideal for a snack or light lunch.

INGREDIENTS

Serves 4–6

4 skinned, boneless chicken breasts
2 garlic cloves, crushed and
   coarsely chopped
2 tablespoons soy sauce
2 tablespoons vegetable oil
½ cup coconut cream
2 tablespoons fish sauce
juice of 1 lime
2 tablespoons palm sugar
4 ounces water chestnuts, sliced
½ cup cashews, toasted
4 shallots, finely sliced
4 kaffir lime leaves, finely sliced
1 lemongrass stalk, finely sliced
1 teaspoon chopped galangal
1 large red chili, seeded and
   finely sliced
2 scallions, finely sliced
10–12 mint leaves, torn
1 head of lettuce, to serve
sprigs of cilantro and 2 green or red
   chilies, seeded and sliced, to garnish

1 Trim the chicken breasts of any excess fat and put them in a large dish. Rub with the garlic, soy sauce and 1 tablespoon of the oil. Allow to marinate for 1–2 hours.

2 Broil or pan-fry the chicken for 3–4 minutes on both sides or until cooked. Remove and set aside to cool.

3 In a small saucepan, heat the coconut cream, fish sauce, lime juice and palm sugar. Stir until all of the sugar has dissolved and then remove from the heat.

4 Cut the cooked chicken into strips and combine with the water chestnuts, cashews, shallots, kaffir lime leaves, lemongrass, galangal, red chili, scallions and mint leaves.

5 Pour the coconut dressing over the chicken, toss and mix well. Serve the chicken on a bed of lettuce leaves and garnish with sprigs of cilantro and sliced chilies.

Noodles with Pineapple, Ginger and Chilies

INGREDIENTS

Serves 4

10 ounces dried udon noodles
½ pineapple, peeled, cored and sliced
    into 1½-inch rings
3 tablespoons light brown sugar
4 tablespoons fresh lime juice
4 tablespoons coconut milk
2 tablespoons fish sauce
2 tablespoons finely grated fresh ginger
2 garlic cloves, finely chopped
1 ripe mango or 2 peaches,
    finely diced
freshly ground black pepper
2 scallions, finely sliced, 2 red chilies,
    seeded and finely shredded,
    plus mint leaves, to garnish

2 Place the pineapple rings in a flameproof dish, sprinkle with 2 tablespoons of the sugar, and broil for 5 minutes or until golden brown. Cool slightly, and cut into small dice.

4 Add the mango or peaches, and toss. Sprinkle over the scallions, chilies and mint leaves before serving.

1 Cook the noodles in a large saucepan of boiling water until tender, following the directions on the package. Drain, refresh under cold water, and drain again.

3 Mix the lime juice, coconut milk and fish sauce in a salad bowl. Add the remaining brown sugar, with the ginger and garlic, and whisk well. Add the noodles and pineapple.

Buckwheat Noodles with Smoked Salmon

Young pea sprouts are only available for a short time. You can substitute watercress, mustard cress, young leeks or your favorite green vegetable or herb in this dish.

INGREDIENTS

Serves 4

8 ounces buckwheat or soba noodles
1 tablespoon oyster sauce
juice of ½ lemon
2–3 tablespoons light olive oil
4 ounces smoked salmon, cut into
    fine strips
4 ounces young pea sprouts
2 ripe tomatoes, peeled, seeded and cut
    into strips
1 tablespoon snipped chives
salt and freshly ground black pepper

1 Cook the buckwheat or soba noodles in a large saucepan of boiling water, following the directions on the package. Drain, rinse under cold running water, and drain again.

2 Turn the noodles into a large bowl. Add the oyster sauce and lemon juice, and season with pepper to taste. Moisten with the olive oil.

3 Add the smoked salmon, pea sprouts, tomatoes and chives. Mix well, and serve at once.

Sesame Duck and Noodle Salad

This salad is complete in itself and makes a lovely summer lunch. The marinade is a marvelous blend of spices.

INGREDIENTS

Serves 4

2 duck breasts
1 tablespoon vegetable oil
2 medium carrots, cut into 3-inch sticks
5 ounces sugar snap peas
8 ounces medium egg noodles
6 scallions, sliced
salt
fresh cilantro leaves, to garnish

For the marinade

1 tablespoon sesame oil
1 teaspoon ground coriander
1 teaspoon Chinese five-spice powder

For the dressing

1 tablespoon garlic vinegar
1 teaspoon light brown sugar
1 teaspoon soy sauce
1 tablespoon toasted sesame seeds
freshly ground black pepper
3 tablespoons sunflower oil
2 tablespoons sesame oil

1 Slice the duck breasts thinly crosswise and place them in a shallow dish. Combine the ingredients for the marinade, pour over the duck and mix well to coat thoroughly. Cover and let sit in a cool place for 30 minutes.

2 Heat the oil in a preheated wok or frying pan, add the slices of duck breast and stir-fry for 3–4 minutes, or until cooked. Set aside.

3 Bring a saucepan of lightly salted water to a boil. Place the carrots and sugar snap peas in a steamer that will fit on top of the pan. When the water boils, add the noodles, place the steamer on top and steam the vegetables while cooking the noodles

for the time suggested on the package. Set the steamed vegetables aside. Drain the noodles, refresh them under cold running water and drain again. Place them in a large serving bowl.

4 To make the dressing, mix the vinegar, sugar, soy sauce and sesame seeds in a bowl. Season well with black pepper, then whisk in the sunflower and sesame oils.

5 Pour the dressing over the noodles and mix well. Add the sugar snap peas, carrots, scallions and duck slices and toss to combine. Scatter the cilantro leaves on top and serve.

Duck, Avocado and Raspberry Salad

Rich duck breasts are roasted until crisp with a honey and soy glaze to serve warm with fresh raspberries and avocado. A delicious raspberry and red currant dressing adds a wonderful sweet-and-sour flavor.

INGREDIENTS

Serves 4

4 small or 2 large duck breasts, halved if large
1 tablespoon honey
1 tablespoon dark soy sauce
4 tablespoons olive oil
1 tablespoon raspberry vinegar
1 tablespoon red currant jelly
selection of salad greens, such as lamb's lettuce, red chicory and frisée
2 avocados, pitted, peeled and cut into chunks
4 ounces raspberries
salt and freshly ground black pepper

1 Prick the skin of each duck breast with a fork. Blend the honey and soy sauce together in a small bowl, then brush all over the skin.

2 Place the duck breasts on a rack set over a roasting pan and season with salt and pepper. Roast in a preheated oven at 425°F for 15–20 minutes, or until the skin is crisp and the meat is cooked.

3 Meanwhile, to make the dressing, put the oil, vinegar, red currant jelly and seasoning in a small bowl and whisk well until evenly blended.

4 Slice the duck breasts diagonally and arrange on individual plates with the salad greens, avocado chunks and raspberries. Spoon the dressing on top and serve immediately.

Spicy Szechuan Noodles

INGREDIENTS

Serves 4
12 ounces thick noodles
6 ounces cooked chicken, shredded
2 ounces roasted cashews

For the dressing
4 scallions, chopped
2 tablespoons chopped cilantro
2 garlic cloves, chopped
2 tablespoons smooth peanut butter
2 tablespoons sweet chili sauce
1 tablespoon soy sauce
1 tablespoon sherry vinegar
1 tablespoon sesame oil
2 tablespoons olive oil
2 tablespoons chicken broth or water
10 toasted Szechuan peppercorns,
    ground

1 Cook the noodles in a saucepan of boiling water until just tender, following the directions on the package. Drain, rinse under cold running water, and drain well.

2 While the noodles are cooking, combine all the ingredients for the dressing in a large bowl. Whisk together well.

3 Add the noodles, shredded chicken and cashews to the dressing, toss gently to coat, and adjust the seasoning to taste. Serve at once.

VARIATION
For a change, you could substitute cooked turkey or pork for the chicken.

Sesame Noodles with Scallions

This simple, but very tasty, warm salad can be prepared and cooked in just a few minutes.

INGREDIENTS

Serves 4
2 garlic cloves, coarsely chopped
2 tablespoons Chinese sesame paste
1 tablespoon dark sesame oil
2 tablespoons soy sauce
2 tablespoons rice wine
1 tablespoon honey
pinch of five-spice powder
12 ounces soba or buckwheat noodles
4 scallions, finely sliced diagonally
2 ounces bean sprouts
3-inch piece of cucumber, cut
    into matchsticks
toasted sesame seeds
salt and freshly ground black pepper

1 Process the garlic, sesame paste, oil, soy sauce, rice wine, honey and five-spice powder with a pinch each of salt and pepper in a blender or food processor until smooth.

2 Cook the noodles in a saucepan of boiling water until just tender, following the directions on the package. Drain the noodles, and turn them into a bowl.

3 Toss the hot noodles with the dressing and the scallions. Top with the bean sprouts, cucumber and sesame seeds, and serve.

COOK'S TIP
If you can't find Chinese sesame paste, then use either tahini or smooth peanut butter instead.

Sweet-and-Sour Fruit and Vegetable Salad

With its clean taste and bright, jewellike colors, *acar bening* makes a perfect accompaniment to many spicy dishes. Any leftover salad can be covered and stored in the refrigerator for up to two days. This is an ideal dish for buffets.

INGREDIENTS

Serves 8
1 small cucumber
salt
1 onion
1 small ripe pineapple or 1 can
  (15 ounces) pineapple rings
1 green bell pepper, thinly sliced
3 firm tomatoes, cut into wedges
3–4 tablespoons cider vinegar or white
  wine vinegar
½ cup water
1 ounce light brown sugar

1 Peel the cucumber and cut in half lengthwise. Remove the seeds with a small spoon. Cut the cucumber into even-sized pieces. Sprinkle with a little salt. Thinly slice the onion and sprinkle with a little salt as well. Let cucumber and onion sit for a few minutes, then rinse and pat dry, and mix them together in a bowl.

2 Peel the fresh pineapple, if using, removing all the "eyes." Slice the pineapple thinly, then core the slices and cut into neat pieces. If using canned pineapple, cut the rings into similar-sized pieces. Add them to the bowl, together with the green bell pepper slices and tomato wedges.

3 Heat the vinegar, water and sugar until the sugar dissolves. Remove from the heat and let cool. When cool, add salt to taste and then pour over the fruit and vegetables. Cover and chill until required.

Rice Vermicelli and Salad Spring Rolls

Goi Cuor is a hearty noodle salad wrapped in rice sheets. It makes a healthy change from a sandwich and is great for a picnic.

INGREDIENTS

Makes 8
2 ounces rice vermicelli, soaked in warm water until soft
1 large carrot, shredded
1 tablespoon sugar
1–2 tablespoons fish sauce
8 x 8-inch round rice sheets
8 large lettuce leaves, thick stalks removed
12 ounces Chinese roast pork, sliced
4 ounces bean sprouts
handful of mint leaves
8 cooked jumbo shrimp, peeled, deveined and halved
½ cucumber, cut into fine strips
cilantro leaves, to garnish

For the peanut sauce
1 tablespoon vegetable oil
3 garlic cloves, finely chopped
1–2 red chilies, finely chopped
1 teaspoon tomato paste
½ cup water
1 tablespoon smooth peanut butter
2 tablespoons hoisin sauce
½ teaspoon sugar
juice of 1 lime
½ cup roasted peanuts, ground

1 Drain the noodles. Cook in a saucepan of boiling water for about 2–3 minutes until tender. Drain, rinse under cold running water, and drain well. Turn into a bowl. Add the carrot. Season with the sugar and fish sauce.

2 Assemble the rolls, one at a time. Dip a rice sheet in a bowl of warm water, then lay it flat on a surface. Place 1 lettuce leaf, 1–2 scoops of the noodle mixture, a few slices of pork, some of the bean sprouts and several mint leaves on the rice sheet.

3 Start rolling up the rice sheet into a cylinder. When half the sheet has been rolled up, fold both sides of the sheet towards the center, and lay 2 pieces of shrimp along the crease.

4 Add a few of strips of cucumber and some of the cilantro leaves. Continue to roll up the sheet to make a tight package. Place the roll on a plate, and cover with a damp dish towel, so that it stays moist while you make the remaining rolls.

5 Make the peanut sauce. Heat the oil in a small saucepan, and fry the garlic, chilies and tomato paste for about 1 minute. Add the water, and bring to a boil, then stir in the peanut butter, hoisin sauce, sugar and lime juice. Mix well. Reduce the heat, and simmer for 3–4 minutes. Spoon the sauce into a bowl, add the ground peanuts, and cool to room temperature.

6 To serve, cut each roll in half. Add a spoonful of the peanut sauce.

Fruit and Raw Vegetable Gado-gado

A banana leaf, which can be
bought from oriental stores, can
be used to line the platter for a
special occasion.

INGREDIENTS

Serves 6

2 unripe pears, peeled at the last
moment, or 6-ounce wedge
bangkuang (yambean), peeled and cut
in matchsticks
1–2 eating apples
juice of ½ lemon
1 small, crisp lettuce, shredded
½ cucumber, seeded, sliced and salted,
set aside for 15 minutes, then rinsed
and drained
6 small tomatoes, cut in wedges
3 slices fresh pineapple, cored and cut
in wedges
3 eggs or 12 quail's eggs, hard-boiled
and shelled
6 ounces egg noodles, cooked, cooled
and chopped
deep-fried onions, to garnish

For the peanut sauce

2–4 fresh red chilies, seeded and
ground
1¼ cups coconut milk
12 ounces crunchy peanut butter
1 tablespoon dark soy sauce or dark
brown sugar
1 teaspoon tamarind pulp, soaked in
3 tablespoons warm water, strained
and juice reserved
coarsely crushed peanuts
salt

1 To make the Peanut Sauce, put the
chilies and coconut milk in a pan.
Add the peanut butter and heat gently,
stirring, until no lumps of peanut
butter remain.

2 Allow to simmer gently until the
sauce thickens, then add the soy
sauce or sugar and tamarind juice.
Season with salt to taste. Pour into a
bowl and sprinkle with a few coarsely
crushed peanuts.

3 To make the salad, peel and core
the pears or *bangkuang* and apples.
Slice the apples and sprinkle with
lemon juice. Arrange the salad and fruit
attractively on a flat platter. The lettuce
can be used, instead of a banana leaf, to
form a bed for the salad.

4 Add the sliced or quartered hard-
cooked eggs (leave quail's eggs
whole), the chopped noodles and the
deep-fried onions.

5 Serve at once, accompanied with a
bowl of the Peanut Sauce.

Sesame Noodle Salad with Hot Peanuts

An Eastern-inspired salad with crunchy vegetables and a light soy dressing.

INGREDIENTS

Serves 4
12 ounces egg noodles
2 medium carrots, cut into fine
    julienne strips
½ cucumber, peeled, seeded and cut
    into ½-inch cubes
4 ounces celery root, peeled and cut
    into fine julienne strips
6 scallions, finely sliced
8 canned water chestnuts, drained and
    finely sliced
6 ounces bean sprouts
1 small fresh green chili, seeded and
    finely chopped
2 tablespoons sesame seeds and 1 cup
    peanuts, to serve

For the dressing
1 tablespoon dark soy sauce
1 tablespoon light soy sauce
1 tablespoon clear honey
1 tablespoon Chinese rice wine or
    dry sherry
1 tablespoon sesame oil

1 Cook the egg noodles in boiling water, following the instructions on the package.

2 Drain the noodles, refresh in cold water, then drain again. Mix the noodles together with all of the prepared vegetables.

3 Combine the dressing ingredients in a small bowl, then toss into the noodle and vegetable mixture. Divide the salad among four plates.

4 Place the sesame seeds and peanuts on separate baking sheets and place in a preheated oven at 400°F. Take the sesame seeds out after 5 minutes and continue to cook the peanuts for another 5 minutes, or until evenly browned.

5 Sprinkle the sesame seeds and peanuts evenly over each salad portion and serve immediately.

Thai Fruit and Vegetable Salad

This fruit salad is typically presented with the main course and serves as a cooler to counteract the heat of Thai curry.

INGREDIENTS

Serves 4–6

1 small pineapple
1 small mango, peeled, pitted
 and sliced
1 green apple, cored and sliced
6 ramboutans or lychees, peeled
 and pitted
4 ounces green beans, halved
1 medium red onion, sliced
1 small cucumber, cut into short sticks
4 ounces bean sprouts
2 scallions, sliced
1 ripe tomato, quartered
8 ounces romaine, Bibb or iceberg
 lettuce leaves, torn into pieces
salt

For the coconut dipping sauce

6 tablespoons coconut cream
2 tablespoons sugar
5 tablespoons boiling water
¼ teaspoon chili sauce
1 tablespoon fish sauce
juice of 1 lime

1 To make the dipping sauce, place the coconut cream, sugar and boiling water in a screw-top jar. Add the chili sauce, fish sauce and lime juice and shake to mix. Set aside.

2 Trim both ends of the pineapple with a serrated knife, then cut away the skin. Remove the central core with an apple corer, or cut the pineapple into four pieces down the middle and remove the core with a knife. Roughly chop the pineapple and set aside with the other fruits.

3 Bring a small saucepan of lightly salted water to a boil and cook the beans for 3–4 minutes. Refresh under cold running water and set aside. To serve, arrange the fruits, vegetables and lettuce leaves in individual heaps in a serving bowl. Serve the dipping sauce separately.

COOK'S TIP

The ramboutan or rambutan, cousin to the lychee, originated in Malaysia but is now cultivated in much of Southeast Asia and the US. It has a dark reddish-brown, hairy skin with sweet, translucent flesh and an inedible pit. It is about two inches in diameter.

Bamboo Shoot Salad

This salad, which has a hot and sharp flavor, originated in northeast Thailand. Use fresh young bamboo shoots when you can find them, otherwise substitute canned bamboo shoots.

INGREDIENTS

Serves 4

14-ounce can whole bamboo shoots
1 ounce glutinous (sticky) rice
2 tablespoons chopped shallots
1 tablespoon chopped garlic
3 tablespoons chopped scallions
2 tablespoons fish sauce
2 tablespoons lime juice
1 teaspoon sugar
½ teaspoon dried flaked chillies
20–25 small mint leaves
1 tablespoon toasted sesame seeds

3 Turn the rice into a bowl, add the shallots, garlic, scallions, fish sauce, lime juice, sugar, chilies and half the mint leaves.

4 Mix thoroughly, then pour over the bamboo shoots and toss together. Serve sprinkled with sesame seeds and the remaining mint leaves.

1 Rinse and drain the bamboo shoots, finely slice and set aside.

2 Dry-roast the rice in a frying pan until it is golden brown. Remove and grind to fine crumbs with a mortar and pestle.

Egg Pancake Salad Wrappers

One of Indonesia's favorite snack foods, pancakes are assembled according to taste and dipped in various sauces.

INGREDIENTS

Makes 12

2 eggs
½ teaspoon salt
1 teaspoon vegetable oil, plus extra
 for frying
1 cup flour
1¼ cups water
shredded lettuce leaves, bean sprouts,
 cucumber wedges, shredded scallions,
 cooked peeled shrimp and cilantro
 sprigs, to serve

For the filling

3 tablespoons vegetable oil
½-inch piece fresh ginger, chopped
1 garlic clove, crushed
1 small red fresh chili, seeded and finely
 chopped
1 tablespoon rice vinegar or white
 wine vinegar
2 teaspoons sugar
4 ounces daikon, grated
1 medium carrot, grated
4 ounces Chinese cabbage, shredded
2 shallots or 1 small red onion,
 thinly sliced

1 Break the eggs into a bowl and stir in the salt, vegetable oil and flour until smooth; do not overmix. Add the water, a little at a time, and strain into a pitcher. Allow the batter to stand for 15–20 minutes before use.

2 Moisten a small, nonstick frying pan with vegetable oil and heat. Pour in enough batter just to cover the base of the pan and cook for 30 seconds. Turn over and cook the other side briefly. Stack the pancakes on a plate, cover and keep warm.

3 To make the filling, heat the oil in a preheated wok, add the ginger, garlic and chili and stir-fry for 1–2 minutes. Add the vinegar, sugar, daikon, carrot, Chinese cabbage and shallots or onion. Cook for 3–4 minutes. Serve with the pancakes, shrimp and salad ingredients.

Green Vegetable Salad with Coconut Mint Dip

This dish is usually served as an accompaniment to Singapore and Malaysian meat dishes.

INGREDIENTS

Serves 4–6

4 ounces snow peas, halved
4 ounces green beans, halved
½ cucumber, peeled, halved and sliced
4 ounces Chinese cabbage, roughly
  shredded
4 ounces bean sprouts
salt
lettuce leaves, to serve

For the dressing

1 garlic clove, crushed
1 small fresh green chili, seeded and
  finely chopped
2 teaspoons sugar
3 tablespoons creamed coconut
5 tablespoons boiling water
2 teaspoons fish sauce
3 tablespoons vegetable oil
juice of 1 lime
2 tablespoons chopped fresh mint

2 To make the dressing, pound the garlic, chili and sugar together in a mortar with a pestle. Add the coconut, boiling water, fish sauce, vegetable oil, lime juice and mint. Stir well.

3 Arrange the blanched vegetables, Chinese cabbage and bean sprouts on a bed of lettuce in a basket, pour the dressing into a shallow bowl and serve.

1 Bring a saucepan of lightly salted water to a boil. Blanch the snow peas, green beans and cucumber for 4 minutes. Drain and refresh under cold running water. Drain and set aside.

Hot Coconut Shrimp and Papaya Salad

This Thai dish may be served as an accompaniment to beef and chicken dishes or on its own as a light lunch in the summer.

INGREDIENTS

Serves 4–6

8 ounces jumbo shrimp, raw or cooked, peeled and deveined
2 ripe papayas
8 ounces mixed salad greens, such as romaine, iceberg or Bibb lettuce, Chinese cabbage or young spinach
1 firm tomato, seeded and roughly chopped
3 scallions, cut into fine strips

For the dressing

1 tablespoon creamed coconut
2 tablespoons boiling water
6 tablespoons vegetable oil
juice of 1 lime
½ teaspoon hot chili sauce
2 teaspoons fish sauce (optional)
1 teaspoon sugar
1 small bunch fresh cilantro, roughly chopped

2 If using raw shrimp, place them in a saucepan and cover with water. Bring to a boil and simmer for 2 minutes. Drain and set aside.

3 To prepare the papaya, cut each in half from top to bottom and remove the black seeds with a teaspoon. Peel away the outer skin and cut the flesh into even-sized pieces. Wash the salad greens and toss in a bowl. Add the other ingredients, pour the dressing on top and serve.

1 First make the dressing: place the creamed coconut in a screw-top jar and add the boiling water. Add the vegetable oil, lime juice, chili sauce, fish sauce, if using, sugar and cilantro. Shake well and set aside, but do not refrigerate.

Eggplant Salad with Dried Shrimp and Egg

An appetizing and unusual salad that you will find yourself making over and over again.

INGREDIENTS

Serves 4–6

2 eggplant
1 tablespoon oil
2 tablespoons dried shrimp, soaked
   and drained
1 tablespoon coarsely chopped garlic
2 tablespoons fresh lime juice
1 teaspoon palm sugar
2 tablespoons fish sauce
1 hard-cooked egg, shelled and
   chopped
4 shallots, finely sliced into rings
cilantro leaves, to garnish
2 red chilies, seeded and sliced,
   to garnish

COOK'S TIP

For an interesting variation, try using salted
duck or quail eggs, cut in halves.

1 Broil or roast the eggplant until charred and tender.

2 When cool enough to handle, peel away the skin and slice the flesh.

3 Heat the oil in a small frying pan, add the drained shrimp and garlic and fry until golden. Remove from the pan and set aside.

4 To make the dressing, put the lime juice, palm sugar and fish sauce in a small bowl and whisk together.

5 To serve, arrange the eggplant on a serving dish. Top with the egg, shallots and dried shrimp mixture. Drizzle over the dressing and garnish with cilantro and red chilies.

NOODLES

*Noodles are the original "fast food"
throughout Asia and are eaten on almost
every possible occasion, from weddings to
funerals. There are numerous varieties
and they are served both hot and cold,
cooked in combination with vegetables,
meat, poultry and seafood. They can be
braised, deep-fried and stir-fried, as well
as made into nests and cakes. Noodles
may be served as a complete meal or as
a side dish. Recipes here include
Singapore Noodles, Seafood Chow
Mein, Special Fried Noodles and Crisp
Pork Meatballs Laced with Noodles.*

Asian Vegetable Noodles

Thin Italian egg pasta is a good
alternative to Asian egg noodles;
use it fresh or dried.

INGREDIENTS

Serves 6

1¼ pounds thin tagliarini
4 ounces shiitake mushrooms
1 red onion
3 tablespoons sesame oil
3 tablespoons dark soy sauce
1 tablespoon balsamic vinegar
2 teaspoons superfine sugar
salt
celery leaves, to garnish

1 Cook the tagliarini in a large pan
of salted boiling water, following
the instructions on the package.

2 Thinly slice the mushrooms and
the red onion, using a sharp knife.

3 Heat 1 tablespoon of the sesame oil
in a preheated wok. When the oil is
hot, stir-fry the onion and mushrooms
for 2 minutes.

4 Drain the tagliarini, then add to
the wok with the soy sauce,
balsamic vinegar, sugar and salt to taste.
Stir-fry for 1 minute, then add the
remaining sesame oil and serve
garnished with celery leaves.

Lettuce Wraps with Sesame Noodles

INGREDIENTS

Serves 4

1 tablespoon vegetable oil
2 duck breasts, about 8 ounces
   each, trimmed
4 tablespoons saké
4 tablespoons soy sauce
2 tablespoons mirin
1 tablespoon sugar
½ cucumber, halved, seeded and
   finely diced
2 tablespoons chopped red onion
2 red chilies, seeded and
   finely chopped
2 tablespoons rice vinegar
4 ounces rice vermicelli, soaked in
   warm water until soft
1 tablespoon dark sesame oil
1 tablespoon black sesame
   seeds, toasted
handful of cilantro leaves
12–16 large green or red
   lettuce leaves
handful of mint leaves
salt and freshly ground black pepper

1 Heat the oil in a large frying pan, add the duck breasts, skin side down, and fry until golden. Turn each breast and fry the other side briefly. Remove the duck, rinse under hot water to remove excess oil, then drain.

2 Combine the saké, soy sauce, mirin and sugar in a saucepan large enough to hold both duck breasts in a single layer. Bring to a boil, add the duck, skin side down, lower the heat, and simmer for 3–5 minutes, depending on the thickness of the duck. Remove the pan from the heat. Let the duck cool in the liquid.

3 Using a slotted spoon, transfer the duck to a board. Then slice thinly using a large, sharp knife. Return the pan to a low heat, and cook the sauce until it reduces and thickens slightly.

4 In a serving bowl, mix the diced cucumber with the red onion, chilies and rice vinegar. Set aside.

5 Cook the noodles in a saucepan of boiling water for about 3 minutes or until tender. Drain and rinse under cold running water. Drain again, then pour into a serving bowl. Toss lightly with the sesame oil and seeds. Season with salt and pepper.

6 Place the thickened sauce and cilantro leaves in separate serving bowls, alongside the bowls of noodles and the cucumber mixture. Arrange the lettuce leaves and sliced duck on individual serving plates.

7 To serve, place a few slices of duck, some noodles, cucumber, herbs and sauce inside a lettuce leaf. Wrap and eat.

Soft Fried Noodles

This is a basic dish for serving as an accompaniment or for those occasions when you are feeling a little out of sorts and just want something simple. Break an egg into the noodles if you want to add protein. They are also good tossed with oyster sauce and a dollop of chili black bean sauce.

INGREDIENTS

Serves 4–6
12 ounces dried egg noodles
2 tablespoons vegetable oil
2 tablespoons finely chopped scallions
soy sauce, to taste
salt and freshly ground black pepper

1 Cook the noodles in a large saucepan of boiling water until just tender, following the directions on the package. Drain, rinse under cold running water, and drain again.

2 Heat the oil in a wok, and swirl it around. Add the scallions, and fry for 30 seconds. Add the noodles, stirring gently to separate the strands.

3 Reduce the heat, and fry the noodles until they are heated through, lightly browned and crisp on the outside, but still soft inside.

4 Season with soy sauce, salt and pepper. Serve at once.

Egg Fried Noodles

Yellow bean sauce gives these noodles a savory flavor.

INGREDIENTS

Serves 4–6
12 ounces medium-thick egg noodles
4 tablespoons vegetable oil
4 scallions, cut into ½-inch rounds
juice of 1 lime
1 tablespoon soy sauce
2 garlic cloves, finely chopped
6 ounces skinless, boneless chicken breast, sliced
6 ounces raw shrimp, peeled and deveined
6 ounces squid, cleaned and cut into rings
1 tablespoon yellow bean sauce
1 tablespoon fish sauce
1 tablespoon light brown sugar
2 eggs
cilantro leaves, to garnish

1 Cook the noodles in a saucepan of boiling water until just tender, then drain well. Set aside.

2 Heat half the oil in a wok or large frying pan. Add the scallions, stir-fry for 2 minutes, then add the noodles, lime juice and soy sauce. Stir-fry for 2–3 minutes. Transfer the mixture to a bowl, and keep warm.

3 Heat the remaining oil in the wok or pan. Add the garlic, chicken, shrimp and squid. Stir-fry over a high heat until cooked.

4 Stir in the yellow bean paste, fish sauce and sugar, then break the eggs into the mixture, stirring gently until they set.

5 Add the noodles, toss lightly to mix, and heat through. Serve garnished with cilantro leaves.

Peanut Noodles

Add any of your favorite vegetables to this recipe to make a great, quick midweek supper—and increase the chili, if you can take the heat!

INGREDIENTS

Serves 4
7 ounces medium egg noodles
2 tablespoons olive oil
2 garlic cloves, crushed
1 large onion, roughly chopped
1 red bell pepper, seeded and roughly chopped
1 yellow bell pepper, seeded and roughly chopped
12 ounces zucchini, roughly chopped
1¼ cups roasted unsalted peanuts, roughly chopped

For the dressing
¼ cup olive oil
grated rind and juice of 1 lemon
1 fresh red chili, seeded and finely chopped
4 tablespoons chopped fresh chives
1–2 tablespoons balsamic vinegar
salt and freshly ground black pepper

1 Cook the noodles according to the package instructions and drain well.

2 Meanwhile, heat the oil in a preheated wok or very large frying pan and cook the garlic and onion for 3 minutes, or until beginning to soften. Add the bell peppers and zucchini and cook for another 15 minutes over medium heat, until beginning to soften and brown. Add the peanuts and cook for 1 minute more.

3 For the dressing, whisk together the olive oil, grated lemon rind and 3 tablespoons lemon juice, the chili, 3 tablespoons of the chives, plenty of seasoning and balsamic vinegar to taste.

4 Toss the noodles into the vegetables and stir-fry to heat through. Add the dressing, stir to coat and serve immediately, garnished with the remaining chopped fresh chives.

Singapore Noodles

Dried Chinese mushrooms add an intense flavor to this lightly curried dish.

INGREDIENTS

Serves 4
¾ ounce dried Chinese mushrooms
8 ounces fine egg noodles
2 teaspoons sesame oil
3 tablespoons peanut oil
2 garlic cloves, crushed
1 small onion, chopped
1 fresh green chili, seeded and
  thinly sliced
2 teaspoons curry powder
4 ounces green beans, halved
4 ounces Chinese cabbage, thinly
  shredded
4 scallions, sliced
2 tablespoons soy sauce
4 ounces cooked jumbo shrimp, peeled
  and deveined
salt

1 Place the mushrooms in a bowl. cover with warm water and soak for 30 minutes. Drain, reserving 2 tablespoons of the soaking water, then slice.

2 Bring a saucepan of lightly salted water to a boil and cook the noodles according to the directions on the package. Drain, transfer to a bowl and toss with the sesame oil.

COOK'S TIP

This dish lends itself to a variety of vegetables. Try snow peas, broccoli, bell peppers or baby corn. The shrimp can be omitted or replaced with ham or chicken, if desired.

3 Heat the peanut oil in a preheated wok. When it is hot, stir-fry the garlic, onion and chili for 3 minutes. Stir in the curry powder and cook for 1 minute. Add the mushrooms, green beans, Chinese cabbage and scallions. Stir-fry for 3–4 minutes, or until the vegetables are tender but still crisp.

4 Add the noodles, soy sauce, reserved mushroom soaking water and shrimp. Toss over the heat for 2–3 minutes, or until the noodles and shrimp are heated through.

Chinese Mushrooms with Cellophane Noodles

Red fermented bean curd adds extra flavor to this hearty vegetarian dish. It is brick-red in color, with a very strong flavor of cheese, and is made by fermenting bean curd (tofu) with salt, red rice and rice wine. Look out for it in cans or jars at Chinese food markets.

INGREDIENTS

Serves 4
4 ounces dried Chinese mushrooms
1 ounce dried wood ears
4 ounces dried bean curd
2 tablespoons vegetable oil
2 garlic cloves, finely chopped
2 slices fresh ginger, finely chopped
10 Szechuan peppercorns, crushed
1 tablespoon red fermented bean curd
½ star anise
pinch of sugar
1–2 tablespoons soy sauce
2 ounces cellophane noodles, soaked in
    hot water until soft
salt

1 Soak the Chinese mushrooms and wood ears separately in bowls of hot water for 30 minutes. Break the dried bean curd into small pieces, and soak in water according to the instructions on the package.

COOK'S TIP

If you can't find Szechuan peppercorns, then use ordinary black ones instead.

2 Strain the mushrooms, reserving the liquid. Squeeze as much liquid from the mushrooms as possible, then discard the mushroom stems. Cut the cups in half if they are large.

3 The wood ears should swell to five times their original size. Drain, rinse thoroughly, and drain again. Cut off any gritty parts, and cut each wood ear into two or three pieces.

4 Heat the oil in a heavy-bottomed pan. Add the garlic, ginger and Szechuan peppercorns. Fry for a few seconds, then add the mushrooms and red fermented bean curd. Mix lightly, and fry for 5 minutes.

5 Add the reserved mushroom liquid to the pan, with sufficient water to cover the mushrooms completely. Add the star anise, sugar and soy sauce, then cover, and simmer for 30 minutes.

6 Add the chopped wood ears and reconstituted bean curd pieces to the pan. Cover, and cook for about 10 minutes.

7 Drain the cellophane noodles, add them to the mixture, and cook for 10 minutes more until tender, adding more liquid if necessary. Add salt to taste, and serve.

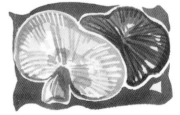

Thai Noodles with Chinese Chives

This recipe requires a little time for preparation but the cooking time is very fast. Everything is cooked speedily in a hot wok and should be eaten at once.

INGREDIENTS

Serves 4
12 ounces dried rice noodles
½-inch piece fresh ginger, grated
2 tablespoons light soy sauce
3 tablespoons vegetable oil
8 ounces firm tofu, cut into small cubes
2 garlic cloves, crushed
1 large onion, cut into thin wedges
4 ounces fried firm tofu, thinly sliced
1 fresh green chili, seeded and
   finely sliced
6 ounces bean sprouts
4 ounces Chinese chives, cut into
   2-inch lengths
2 ounces roasted peanuts, ground
2 tablespoons dark soy sauce
fresh cilantro leaves, to garnish

1 Place the noodles in a large bowl, cover with warm water and soak for 20–30 minutes, then drain. Blend together the ginger, light soy sauce and 1 tablespoon of the oil in a bowl. Stir in the tofu and set aside for 10 minutes. Drain, reserving the marinade.

2 Heat 1 tablespoon of the oil in a preheated wok or frying pan and fry the garlic for a few seconds. Add the tofu and stir-fry for 3–4 minutes. Transfer to a plate and set aside.

3 Heat the remaining oil in the wok or frying pan and stir-fry the onion for 3–4 minutes, or until softened and just beginning to color. Add the fried tofu and chili, stir-fry briefly, and then add the noodles. Stir-fry for 4–5 minutes.

4 Stir in the bean sprouts, Chinese chives and most of the ground peanuts, reserving a little for the garnish. Add the tofu, the dark soy sauce and the reserved marinade.

5 When hot, spoon onto serving plates and garnish with the remaining ground peanuts and cilantro leaves.

COOK'S TIP

Tofu makes this a vegetarian meal, but, thinly sliced pork or chicken could be used instead.

Udon Pot

INGREDIENTS

Serves 4

12 ounces dried udon noodles
1 large carrot, cut into bite-size chunks
8 ounces chicken breasts or thighs,
  skinned and cut into bite-size pieces
8 raw jumbo shrimp, peeled
  and deveined
4–6 Chinese cabbage leaves, cut into
  short strips
8 shiitake mushrooms, stems removed
2 ounces snow peas, ends removed
6¼ cups chicken broth or instant
  bonito broth (dashi)
2 tablespoons mirin
soy sauce, to taste
1 bunch scallions, finely chopped,
  2 tablespoons grated fresh ginger,
  lemon wedges, and extra soy sauce,
  to serve

1 Cook the noodles until just tender, following the directions on the package. Drain, rinse under cold water, and drain again. Blanch the carrot in boiling water for 1 minute, then drain.

2 Spoon the noodles and carrot chunks into a large saucepan or flameproof casserole, and arrange the chicken breasts or thighs, shrimp, Chinese cabbage leaves, mushrooms and snow peas on top.

3 Bring the broth to a boil in a saucepan. Add the mirin and enough soy sauce to taste. Pour the broth over the noodles. Cover the pan or casserole, bring to a boil over a moderate heat, then simmer gently for 5–6 minutes until all the ingredients are cooked.

4 Serve with chopped scallions, grated ginger, lemon wedges and a little soy sauce.

Combination Chow Mein

INGREDIENTS

Serves 4–6

1 pound thick egg noodles
3 tablespoons vegetable oil
2 garlic cloves, chopped
2 scallions, cut into short lengths
2 ounces pork loin, sliced, or Chinese
  roast pork cut into short lengths
2 ounces pork liver, sliced
3 ounces raw shrimp, peeled
  and deveined
2 ounces prepared squid, sliced
2 ounces mussels
4 ounces watercress, leaves stripped
  from the stems
2 red chilies, seeded and finely sliced
2–3 tablespoons soy sauce
1 tablespoon sesame oil
salt and freshly ground black pepper

1 Cook the egg noodles in a large saucepan of boiling water until just tender. Drain thoroughly.

2 Heat the oil in a wok, and fry the garlic and scallions for 30 seconds. Add the pork loin, if using, with the liver, shrimp, squid and mussels. Stir-fry for 2 minutes over a high heat.

3 Add the watercress and chilies, and stir-fry for 3–4 minutes more until the meat is cooked.

4 Add the drained noodles, stirring constantly but gently. Toss in the Chinese roast pork, if using, and add the soy sauce with salt and pepper to taste. Cook until the noodles are thoroughly heated through. Stir in the sesame oil, mix well, and serve.

Cellophane Noodles with Pork

Unlike other types of noodles, cellophane noodles can be reheated successfully.

INGREDIENTS

Serves 3–4

4 ounces cellophane noodles
4 dried Chinese black mushrooms
8 ounces boneless lean pork
2 tablespoons dark soy sauce
2 tablespoons Chinese rice wine or
   dry sherry
2 garlic cloves, crushed
1 tablespoon grated fresh ginger
1 teaspoon chili oil
3 tablespoons peanut oil
4–6 scallions, chopped
1 teaspoon cornstarch blended with
   ¾ cup chicken broth or water
2 tablespoons chopped fresh cilantro
salt and freshly ground black pepper
fresh cilantro sprigs, to garnish

1 Put the noodles and mushrooms in separate bowls and pour in sufficient warm water to cover. Set aside to soak for 15–20 minutes, until soft. Drain well. Cut the noodles into 5-inch lengths using scissors or a knife. Squeeze out any excess water from the mushrooms, discard the stems and finely chop the caps.

2 Cut the pork into very small cubes and place them in a bowl. Add the soy sauce, rice wine or dry sherry, garlic, ginger and chili oil and mix well. Marinate for 15 minutes. Drain, reserving the marinade.

3 Heat the peanut oil in a preheated wok. Add the pork and mushrooms and stir-fry for 3 minutes. Add the scallions and stir-fry for 1 minute. Stir in the cornstarch mixture and reserved marinade and season to taste. Cook for 1 minute.

4 Add the noodles and stir-fry for about 2 minutes, until the noodles have absorbed most of the liquid and the pork is cooked through. Stir in the chopped cilantro. Serve immediately garnished with the cilantro sprigs.

Noodles with Chicken, Shrimp and Ham

Egg noodles can be cooked up to 24 hours in advance and kept in a bowl of cold water.

INGREDIENTS

Serves 4–6

10 ounces dried egg noodles
1 tablespoon vegetable oil
1 medium onion, chopped
1 garlic clove, crushed
1-inch piece fresh ginger, chopped
2 ounces canned water chestnuts, drained and sliced
1 tablespoon light soy sauce
2 tablespoons fish sauce or strong chicken broth
6 ounces cooked chicken breast, sliced
5 ounces cooked ham, thickly sliced and cut into short fingers
8 ounces cooked jumbo shrimp, peeled
6 ounces bean sprouts
7 ounces canned baby corn, drained
2 limes, cut into wedges, and 1 small bunch cilantro, chopped, to garnish

1 Cook the noodles according to the package instructions. Drain well and set aside.

2 Heat the oil in a preheated wok or frying pan. Fry the onion, garlic and ginger for 3 minutes, or until soft but not colored. Add the chestnuts, soy sauce, fish sauce or chicken broth, chicken breast, ham and shrimp.

3 Add the noodles, bean sprouts and baby corn and stir-fry for 6–8 minutes, until heated through. Transfer to a warmed serving dish, garnish with the lime wedges and chopped cilantro and serve immediately.

Seafood Chow Mein

This basic recipe can be adapted using different items for the "dressing."

INGREDIENTS

Serves 4

3 ounces squid, cleaned
3 ounces jumbo shrimp
3–4 fresh scallops
½ egg white
1 tablespoon cornstarch paste
9 ounces egg noodles
5–6 tablespoons vegetable oil
2 ounces snow peas
½ teaspoon salt
½ teaspoon light brown sugar
1 tablespoon Chinese rice wine or
   dry sherry
2 tablespoons light soy sauce
2 scallions, cut into fine strips
Basic Broth, if necessary
few drops of sesame oil

1 Open up the squid and score the inside in a crisscross pattern with a sharp knife. Cut the squid into pieces, each about the size of a postage stamp. Soak the squid in a bowl of boiling water until all the pieces curl up. Rinse in cold water and drain.

2 Peel and devein the shrimp, then cut each in half lengthwise.

3 Prepare the scallops and cut into 3 or 4 slices. Combine the scallops, shrimp, egg white and cornstarch paste.

4 Cook the noodles in boiling water according to the package instructions. Drain and refresh under cold water. Mix with about 1 tablespoon of the oil.

5 Heat 2–3 tablespoons of the oil in a preheated wok. Stir-fry the snow peas, squid and shrimp mixture for about 2 minutes, then add the salt, sugar, rice wine or dry sherry, half the soy sauce and the scallions. Blend well and add a little broth, if necessary. Remove from the wok and keep warm.

6 Heat the remaining oil in the wok and stir-fry the noodles for 2–3 minutes with the remaining soy sauce. Place in a large serving dish, pour the "dressing" on top and sprinkle with a little sesame oil. Serve hot or cold.

Special Fried Noodles

Perhaps the best-known dish of Singapore is *mee goreng*. It is prepared from a wide range of ingredients.

INGREDIENTS

Serves 4–6

10 ounces egg noodles
1 skinless, boneless chicken breast
4 ounces lean pork
2 tablespoons vegetable oil
6 ounces jumbo shrimp, raw or
    cooked, peeled
4 shallots or 1 medium onion, chopped
¾-inch piece fresh ginger, thinly sliced
2 garlic cloves, crushed
3 tablespoons light soy sauce
1-2 teaspoons chili sauce
1 tablespoon rice vinegar or white
    wine vinegar
1 teaspoon sugar
½ teaspoon salt
4 ounces Chinese cabbage, cut into strips
4 ounces spinach, cut into fine strips
3 scallions, cut into fine strips

1 Bring a large saucepan of lightly salted water to a boil and cook the noodles according to the instructions on the package. Drain and set aside. Place the chicken breast and pork in the freezer for 30 minutes to firm, but not freeze.

2 Slice the meat thinly against the grain. Heat the oil in a preheated wok and stir-fry the chicken, pork and shrimp for 2–3 minutes. Add the shallots or onion, ginger and garlic and stir-fry for 2–3 minutes, or until softened but not colored.

3 Add the soy sauce, chili sauce, vinegar, sugar and salt. Bring to a simmer. Add the Chinese cabbage, spinach and scallions, cover and cook for 3–4 minutes. Add the noodles, heat through and serve.

Straw Noodle Shrimp in a Sweet Ginger Dip

Shrimp are a popular feature in Japanese cooking. Rarely are they more delicious than when wrapped in crispy noodles.

INGREDIENTS

Serves 4–6

3 ounces somen noodles or vermicelli
3 sheets nori
12 large jumbo shrimp, peeled and
   deveined
vegetable oil, for deep-frying

For the dipping sauce

6 tablespoons soy sauce
2 tablespoons sugar
¼-inch piece fresh ginger, grated

1 Cover the somen noodles, if using, with boiling water and let soak for 1–2 minutes. Drain and dry thoroughly with paper towels. Cut the noodles into 3-inch lengths. If using vermicelli, cover with boiling water and let soak for 1–2 minutes to soften. Drain and set aside. Cut the nori into ½ x 2-inch strips and set aside.

2 To make the dipping sauce, bring the soy sauce to a boil in a small saucepan with the sugar, then add the ginger. Simmer for 2–3 minutes, strain and set aside to cool.

3 Line up the noodles or vermicelli on a wooden board. Straighten each shrimp by pushing a bamboo skewer through its length. Roll the shrimp in the noodles or vermicelli so that they adhere in neat strands.

4 Moisten one end of the nori strips and secure the noodles at the fat end of each shrimp. Set aside.

5 Heat the vegetable oil in a preheated wok with a wire draining rack or in a deep-fryer to 350°F. Fry the shrimp in the oil, two at a time, until the noodles or vermicelli are crisp and golden.

6 To finish, cut through the band of nori with a sharp knife, exposing a clean section of shrimp. Drain on paper towels and serve with the dipping sauce in a small dish.

Main Course Spicy Shrimp and Noodle Soup

This dish is served as a hot coconut broth with a separate platter of shrimp, fish and noodles. Diners are invited to add their own choice of accompaniment to the broth.

INGREDIENTS

Serves 4–6

¼ cup raw cashews
3 shallots or 1 medium onion, sliced
2-inch piece lemongrass, cut into strips
2 garlic cloves, crushed
5 ounces laksa noodles (spaghetti-sized rice noodles), soaked for 10 minutes before cooking
2 tablespoons vegetable oil
½-inch-square shrimp paste or 1 tablespoon fish sauce
1 tablespoon mild curry paste
1 can (14 ounces) coconut milk
½ chicken bouillon cube
3 curry leaves (optional)
1 pound white fish fillet, such as cod, haddock or whiting
8 ounces jumbo shrimp, raw or cooked, peeled
1 small head romaine lettuce, shredded
4 ounces bean sprouts
3 scallions, cut into fine strips
½ cucumber, sliced and cut into strips
shrimp crackers, to serve

1 Grind the cashews with the shallots or onion, lemongrass and garlic in a mortar with a pestle or in a food processor. Cook the noodles according to the instructions on the package.

2 Heat the oil in a large preheated wok or saucepan, add the cashew mixture and stir-fry for 1–2 minutes, or until the nuts are just beginning to brown.

3 Add the shrimp paste or fish sauce and curry paste, followed by the coconut milk, bouillon cube and curry leaves, if using. Simmer for 10 minutes.

4 Cut the white fish into bite-sized pieces. Add the fish and shrimp to the simmering coconut broth and cook for 3–4 minutes. Remove with a slotted spoon. Set aside.

5 To serve, line a large serving platter with the shredded lettuce leaves. Arrange the bean sprouts, scallions and cucumber in neat piles, together with the fish, shrimp and noodles. Serve the salad with a bowl of shrimp crackers and the broth in a closed-rim stoneware pot.

COOK'S TIP

When cooking the fish and shrimp, you may find it easier to put them in a large frying basket before immersing them in the coconut broth.

Rice Noodles with Beef and Black Bean Sauce

This is an excellent combination – beef with a chili sauce tossed with silky, smooth rice noodles.

INGREDIENTS

Serves 4

1 pound fresh rice noodles
4 tablespoons vegetable oil
1 onion, finely sliced
2 garlic cloves, finely chopped
2 slices fresh ginger, finely chopped
8 ounces mixed bell peppers, seeded and cut into strips
12 ounces round steak, finely sliced against the grain
3 tablespoons fermented black beans, rinsed in warm water, drained and chopped
2 tablespoons soy sauce
2 tablespoons oyster sauce
1 tablespoon chili black bean sauce
1 tablespoon cornstarch
½ cup broth or water
2 scallions, finely chopped, and 2 red chilies, seeded and finely sliced, to garnish

1 Rinse the noodles under hot water. Drain well. Heat half the oil in a wok or large frying pan, swirling it around. Add the onion, garlic, ginger and mixed pepper strips. Stir-fry for 3–5 minutes, then remove with a slotted spoon, and keep hot.

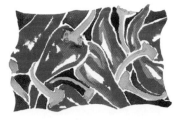

2 Add the remaining oil to the wok. When hot, add the sliced beef and fermented black beans, and stir-fry over a high heat for 5 minutes or until they are cooked.

3 In a small bowl, blend the soy sauce, oyster sauce and chili black bean sauce with the cornstarch and broth or water until smooth. Add the mixture to the wok, then return the onion mixture to the wok and cook, stirring, for 1 minute.

4 Add the noodles, and mix lightly. Stir over a medium heat until the noodles are heated through. Adjust the seasoning, if necessary. Serve at once, garnished with the chopped scallions and chilies.

Crisp Pork Meatballs Laced with Noodles

These little meatballs, decoratively coated with a lacing of noodles, look very impressive but are actually extremely easy to make.

INGREDIENTS

Serves 4

14 ounces ground pork
2 garlic cloves, finely chopped
2 tablespoons chopped fresh cilantro
1 tablespoon oyster sauce
2 tablespoons fresh bread crumbs
1 egg, beaten
6 ounces fresh thin egg noodles
oil, for deep-frying
salt and freshly ground black pepper
fresh cilantro leaves, to garnish
spinach leaves and chili sauce or tomato
    sauce, to serve

1 Combine the pork, garlic, chopped cilantro, oyster sauce, bread crumbs and egg. Season with salt and pepper.

2 Knead the pork mixture until it is sticky, then form into balls each the size of a walnut.

3 Blanch the noodles in a saucepan of boiling water for 2–3 minutes. Drain, rinse under cold running water and drain well.

4 Wrap 3–5 strands of noodles securely around each meatball in a crisscross pattern.

5 Heat the oil in a deep-fryer or preheated wok. Deep-fry the meatballs in batches until golden brown and cooked through to the center. As each batch browns, remove with a slotted spoon and drain well on paper towels. Serve hot on a bed of spinach leaves, garnished with fresh cilantro leaves and with chili sauce or tomato sauce in a small dish on the side.

Noodles, Chicken and Shrimp in Coconut Broth

This typical Indonesian dish has several different components from which the diners may help themselves, making a complete meal in itself.

INGREDIENTS

Serves 8
2 onions, quartered
1-inch piece fresh ginger, sliced
2 garlic cloves
4 macadamia nuts or 8 almonds
1–2 fresh chilies, seeded and sliced
2 lemongrass stems, lower
   2 inches sliced
2-inch piece fresh turmeric, peeled and
   sliced, or 1 teaspoon ground turmeric
1 tablespoon coriander seeds, dry-fried
4 tablespoons sunflower oil
1 can (14 fluid ounces) coconut milk
6¼ cups chicken broth
12 ounces rice noodles, soaked in
   cold water
12 ounces cooked jumbo shrimp,
   peeled and deveined
salt and freshly ground black pepper

For the garnish
4 hard-cooked eggs, shelled and
   quartered
8 ounces cooked chicken, chopped
8 ounces bean sprouts
1 bunch scallions, cut into fine strips
1 onion, finely sliced and deep-fried

1 Place the quartered onions, ginger, garlic and nuts in a food processor with the chilies, lemongrass and turmeric. Process to a paste. Alternatively, pound all the ingredients in a mortar with a pestle. Grind the coriander seeds coarsely and add to the paste.

2 Heat the oil in a preheated wok or frying pan and fry the spice paste, without allowing it to color, to bring out the flavors. Add the coconut milk, broth and seasoning. Simmer for 5–10 minutes.

3 Meanwhile, drain the noodles and plunge them into a large pan of salted boiling water for 2 minutes. Remove from the heat and drain thoroughly. Rinse well with plenty of cold water. Add the jumbo shrimp to the soup just before serving and heat through for a minute or two.

4 Arrange the garnishes in separate bowls. Each person takes a helping of noodles, tops them with soup, eggs, chicken and bean sprouts, then scatters scallions and fried onion on top.

Noodles in Soup

In China, noodles in soup are far more popular than fried noodles. This is a basic recipe, which you can adapt by using different ingredients.

INGREDIENTS

Serves 4

8 ounces skinless, boneless chicken or
  pork loins
3–4 dried Chinese mushrooms, soaked
1 can (4 ounces) bamboo shoots, drained
4 ounces spinach leaves, lettuce hearts
  or Chinese cabbage
2 scallions
12 ounces dried egg noodles
2½ cups Basic Broth
2 tablespoons vegetable oil
1 teaspoon salt
½ teaspoon light brown sugar
1 tablespoon light soy sauce
2 teaspoons Chinese rice wine or
  dry sherry
few drops of sesame oil

1 Thinly slice the meat. Squeeze the mushrooms dry and discard any hard stalks. Thinly slice the mushroom caps, bamboo shoots, spinach, lettuce hearts or Chinese cabbage and the scallions. Keep the meat, the scallions and the other ingredients in three heaps.

2 Cook the noodles in boiling water according to the instructions on the package, then drain and rinse in cold water. Place in a serving bowl.

3 Bring the broth to a boil and pour over the noodles. Keep warm.

4 Heat the oil in a preheated wok, add the scallions and the meat and stir-fry for about 1 minute.

5 Add the mushrooms, bamboo shoots and spinach, lettuce or Chinese cabbage and stir-fry for 1 minute, or until the meat is cooked through. Add the salt, sugar, soy sauce, rice wine or dry sherry and sesame oil and blend well.

6 Pour the "dressing" over the noodles and serve.

RICE DISHES

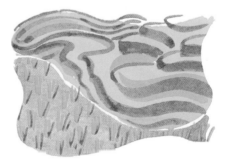

Rice is a staple food throughout much of China and the rest of Asia. While plain boiled rice is a useful accompaniment that goes well with a wide variety of dishes, it is easy to combine rice with vegetables, eggs and a range of flavorings and spices to create a more special meal.

Rice dishes from each country and region have their own unique flavors. Try Chinese Special Fried Rice, Sushi Rice from Japan, Thai Rice with Bean Sprouts or Rice Porridge with Chicken from Indonesia. Don't overlook Coconut Rice Fritters, a sweet snack from the Philippines.

Plain Rice

Use long-grain or *patna* rice, or fragrant rice from Thailand. Allow two ounces raw rice per person. If you use fragrant Thai rice, omit the salt.

INGREDIENTS

Serves 4
generous 1 cup rice
about 1 cup water
pinch of salt
½ teaspoon vegetable oil

1 Wash and rinse the rice. Place the rice in a saucepan and add the water. There should be no more than ¼ inch of water above the surface of the rice.

2 Bring to a boil, add the salt and oil, then stir to prevent the rice from sticking to the bottom of the pan. Reduce the heat to very, very low, cover and cook for 15–20 minutes.

3 Remove from the heat and let stand, still covered, for 10 minutes. Fluff up the rice with a fork or spoon just before serving.

Egg-fried Rice

Use rice with a fairly firm texture. Ideally, the raw rice should be soaked in water for a short time before cooking.

INGREDIENTS

Serves 4
3 eggs
1 teaspoon salt
2 scallions, finely chopped
2–3 tablespoons vegetable oil
1 pound cooked rice
4 ounces frozen peas

1 In a bowl, lightly beat the eggs with a pinch of the salt and a few pieces of scallion.

2 Heat the oil in a preheated wok, and lightly scramble the eggs.

3 Add the cooked rice and stir to make sure that each grain of rice is separated. Add the remaining salt and scallions and the peas. Blend well, allow to heat through and serve.

Chinese Special Fried Rice

This recipe combines a tasty mixture of chicken, shrimp and vegetables with fried rice.

INGREDIENTS

Serves 4

scant 1 cup long-grain white rice
3 tablespoons peanut oil
1½ cups water
1 garlic clove, crushed
4 scallions, finely chopped
4 ounces cooked chicken, diced
4 ounces cooked jumbo shrimp, peeled
2 ounces frozen peas
1 egg, lightly beaten
2 ounces lettuce, shredded
2 tablespoons light soy sauce
pinch of superfine sugar
salt and freshly ground black pepper
1 tablespoon chopped roasted cashews, to garnish

1 Rinse the rice in two to three changes of warm water to wash away some of the starch. Drain well.

2 Put the rice in a saucepan and add 1 tablespoon of the oil and the water. Cover and bring to a boil, stir once, then cover and simmer for 12–15 minutes, until nearly all the water has been absorbed. Turn off the heat and cover; let stand for 10 minutes. Fluff up with a fork and let cool.

3 Heat the remaining oil in a preheated wok or frying pan, add the garlic and scallions and stir-fry for 30 seconds.

4 Add the chicken, shrimp and peas and stir-fry for 1–2 minutes, then add the cooked rice and stir-fry for another 2 minutes. Pour in the egg and stir-fry until just set. Stir in the lettuce, soy sauce, sugar and seasoning.

5 Transfer to a warmed serving bowl, sprinkle with the chopped cashews and serve immediately.

Egg Foo Yung

A great way of turning a bowl of
leftover cooked rice into a meal
for four, this dish is tasty and full
of texture.

INGREDIENTS

Serves 4
3 eggs, beaten
pinch of Chinese five-spice
    powder (optional)
3 tablespoons peanut or
    sunflower oil
4 scallions, sliced
1 garlic clove, crushed
1 small green bell pepper, seeded and
    chopped
4 ounces bean sprouts
generous 1 cup white rice, cooked
3 tablespoons light soy sauce
1 tablespoon sesame oil
salt and freshly ground black pepper

1 Season the eggs with salt and
pepper to taste and beat in the
five-spice powder, if using.

2 Heat 1 tablespoon of the oil in a
preheated wok or large frying pan
and, when quite hot, pour in the eggs.
Cook rather like an omelet, pulling the
mixture away from the sides and
allowing the rest to slip underneath.

3 Cook the egg until firm, then slide
out. Chop the omelet into small
strips and set aside.

4 Heat the remaining oil and stir-fry
the scallions, garlic, green bell pepper
and bean sprouts for about 2 minutes,
stirring and tossing continuously.

5 Combine the cooked rice and heat
thoroughly, stirring well. Add the
soy sauce and sesame oil, then return
the egg strips to the pan and mix in
well. Serve immediately, piping hot.

Malacca Fried Rice

There are many versions of this dish throughout the East, all of which make use of leftover rice. Ingredients vary according to what is available, but shrimp are a popular addition.

INGREDIENTS

Serves 4–6
2 eggs
3 tablespoons vegetable oil
4 shallots or 1 medium onion, finely chopped
1 teaspoon finely chopped fresh ginger
1 garlic clove, crushed
8 ounces jumbo shrimp, raw or cooked, peeled and deveined
1–2 teaspoon chili sauce (optional)
3 scallions, green parts only, roughly chopped
8 ounces frozen peas
8 ounces thickly sliced roast pork, diced
3 tablespoons light soy sauce
1⅔ cups long-grain rice, cooked
salt and freshly ground black pepper

2 Heat the remaining oil in a large preheated wok, add the shallots or onion, ginger, garlic and shrimp and cook for 1–2 minutes, making sure that the garlic does not burn.

3 Add the chili sauce, scallions, peas, pork and soy sauce. Stir to heat through, then add the cooked rice. Fry the rice over moderate heat for 6–8 minutes. Transfer to a dish and decorate with the egg strips.

1 In a bowl, beat the eggs well and season to taste with salt and pepper. Heat 1 tablespoon of the oil in a large, nonstick frying pan, pour in the eggs and cook for about 30 seconds, without stirring, until set. Roll up the omelet, cut into thin strips and set aside.

Asian Fried Rice

This is a great way to use leftover cooked rice. Make sure the rice is very cold before attempting to fry it, as warm rice will become soggy. Some supermarkets sell frozen cooked rice.

INGREDIENTS

Serves 4–6
5 tablespoons oil
4 ounces shallots, halved and thinly
    sliced
3 garlic cloves, crushed
1 red chili, seeded and finely chopped
6 scallions, finely chopped
1 red bell pepper, seeded and finely
    chopped
8 ounces white cabbage, finely
    shredded
6 ounces cucumber, finely chopped
2 ounces frozen peas, thawed
3 eggs, beaten
1 teaspoon tomato paste
2 tablespoons lime juice
¼ teaspoon Tabasco sauce
1½ pounds cooked white rice, cooled
1 cup cashews, roughly chopped
2 tablespoons chopped fresh cilantro,
    plus extra to garnish
salt and freshly ground black pepper

1 Heat the oil in a large preheated wok or nonstick frying pan and cook the shallots until very crisp and golden. Remove with a slotted spoon and drain on paper towels.

2 Add the garlic and chili and cook for 1 minute. Add the scallions and red bell pepper and cook for 3–4 minutes, or until the scallions are beginning to soften.

3 Add the cabbage, cucumber and peas and cook for another 2 minutes.

4 Make a gap in the ingredients in the wok or frying pan and add the beaten eggs. Scramble the eggs, stirring occasionally, and then stir them into the vegetables.

5 Add the tomato paste, lime juice and Tabasco sauce and stir well to combine.

6 Increase the heat and add the cooked rice, cashews, cilantro and plenty of seasoning. Stir-fry for 3–4 minutes, until piping hot. Serve garnished with the crisp shallots and extra fresh cilantro, if desired.

COOK'S TIP

1½ pounds cooked rice is equivalent to 8 ounces raw weight.

Shiitake Fried Rice

Shiitake mushrooms have a strong, meaty aroma and flavor. This is a very easy recipe to make, and although it is a side dish, it can almost be a meal in itself.

Ingredients

Serves 4

2 eggs
1 tablespoon water
3 tablespoons vegetable oil
12 ounces shiitake mushrooms
8 scallions, sliced diagonally
1 garlic clove, crushed
½ green bell pepper, seeded and chopped
3 tablespoons butter
about 1 cup long-grain rice, cooked
1 tablespoon medium-dry sherry
2 tablespoons dark soy sauce
1 tablespoon chopped fresh cilantro
salt

1 Beat the eggs with the water and season with a little salt.

2 Heat 1 tablespoon of the oil in a preheated wok or large frying pan, pour in the eggs and cook to make a large omelet. Lift the sides of the omelet and tilt the wok so that the uncooked egg can run underneath and be cooked. Roll up the omelet and slice thinly.

3 Remove and discard the mushroom stalks, if they are tough. Slice the caps thinly, halving them if they are large.

4 Heat 1 tablespoon of the oil in the wok and stir-fry the scallions and garlic for 3–4 minutes, until softened but not brown. Transfer them to a plate using a slotted spoon and set aside.

5 Add the green bell pepper and stir-fry for about 2–3 minutes, then add the butter and the remaining oil. As the butter begins to sizzle, add the mushrooms and stir-fry over moderate heat for 3–4 minutes, or until both vegetables are soft.

6 Loosen the rice grains as much as possible. Pour the sherry over the mushrooms and then stir in the rice.

7 Heat the rice over moderate heat, stirring all the time to prevent it from sticking. If the rice seems very dry, add a little more oil. Stir in the cooked scallions, garlic and omelet slices, the soy sauce and the chopped cilantro. Cook for a few minutes, until heated through, and serve.

Sushi

INGREDIENTS

Makes 8–10
For the tuna sushi
3 sheets nori (paper-thin seaweed)
5 ounces very-fresh tuna fillet, cut
   into strips
1 teaspoon wasabi paste
6 young carrots, blanched
6 cups cooked Japanese rice

For the salmon sushi
2 eggs
½ teaspoon salt
2 teaspoons sugar
5 sheets nori
6 cups cooked Japanese rice
5 ounces very-fresh salmon fillet, cut
   into fingers
1 teaspoon wasabi paste
½ small cucumber, cut into strips

1 To make the tuna sushi, spread half a sheet of nori onto a bamboo mat, lay strips of tuna across the full length and season with the thinned wasabi. Place a line of blanched carrot next to the tuna and roll tightly. Moisten the edge with water and seal.

2 Place a square of damp waxed paper on the bamboo mat, then spread evenly with sushi rice. Place the non-wrapped tuna along the center and wrap tightly, enclosing the nori completely. Remove the paper and cut into neat rounds with a wet knife.

3 To make the salmon sushi, make a simple flat omelette by beating together the eggs, salt and sugar. Heat a large non-stick pan, pour in the egg mixture, stir briefly and allow to set. Transfer to a clean dish towel and cool.

4 Place the nori on a bamboo mat, cover with the omelette and trim to size. Spread a layer of rice over the omelette, then lay strips of salmon across the width. Season the salmon with the thinned wasabi, then place a strip of cucumber next to the salmon. Fold the bamboo mat in half. Cut into neat rounds with a wet knife.

Coconut Rice Fritters

These delicious fritters from the Philippines can be served at any time and go especially well with coffee or hot chocolate.

INGREDIENTS

Makes 28

⅔ cup long-grain rice, cooked
2 tablespoons coconut milk powder
3 tablespoons sugar
2 egg yolks
juice of ½ lemon
3 ounces shredded coconut
oil, for deep-frying
confectioners' sugar, for dusting

1 Place ⅓ cup of the cooked rice in a mortar and pound with a pestle until smooth and sticky. Alternatively, process in a food processor. Transfer to a bowl and mix in the remaining rice, the coconut milk powder, sugar, egg yolks and lemon juice.

2 Spread out the shredded coconut on a baking sheet or plate. With wet hands, divide the rice mixture into thumb-sized pieces and roll them in the coconut to make neat balls.

3 Heat the oil in a wok or deep-fryer to 350°F. Fry the coconut rice balls, three or four at a time, for 1–2 minutes, until the coconut is evenly browned. Transfer to a plate and dust with confectioners' sugar. Place a wooden skewer in each fritter and serve in the traditional way, as an afternoon snack.

COOK'S TIP

In the Philippines, hot chocolate is made by preparing a syrup with 2 tablespoons sugar and ½ cup water and then melting 4 ounces pieces of best-quality plain chocolate in it. Finally, a scant 1 cup evaporated milk is whisked in over low heat. This luxurious drink serves two.

Thai Rice with Bean Sprouts

Thai rice has a delicate fragrance that is delicious hot or cold.

INGREDIENTS

Serves 6

1 cup Thai fragrant rice
2 tablespoons sesame oil
2 tablespoons fresh lime juice
1 small red chili pepper, seeded and chopped
1 garlic clove, crushed
2 teaspoons grated fresh ginger
2 tablespoons light soy sauce
1 teaspoon honey
3 tablespoons pineapple juice
1 tablespoon wine vinegar
2 green onions, sliced
2 canned pineapple rings, chopped
1¼ cups sprouted lentils or beansprouts
1 small red bell pepper, sliced
1 stalk celery, sliced
½ cup cashew nuts, chopped
2 tablespoons toasted sesame seeds
salt and freshly ground black pepper

1 Soak the Thai fragrant rice for 20 minutes, then rinse in several changes of water. Drain, then boil in salted water for 10–12 minutes until tender. Drain and set aside.

2 In a large bowl, whisk together the sesame oil, lime juice, chili, garlic, ginger, soy sauce, honey, pineapple juice and vinegar. Stir in the rice.

3 Add the green onions, pineapple rings, sprouted lentils or beansprouts, red pepper, celery, cashew nuts and the toasted sesame seeds and mix well. If the rice grains stick together while cooling, simply stir them with a metal spoon. This dish can be served warm or lightly chilled and is a good accompaniment to grilled or barbecued meats and fish.

COOK'S TIP

Sesame oil has a strong, nutty flavor and is good for seasoning, marinating or flavoring rather than for cooking. Because the taste is so distinctive, sesame oil can be mixed with grapeseed or other light-flavored oils.

Coconut Rice

This rich dish is usually served with a tangy papaya salad.

INGREDIENTS

Serves 4–6

2 cups jasmine rice
1 cup water
2 cups unsweetened coconut milk
½ teaspoon salt
2 tablespoons sugar
fresh shredded coconut, to garnish
(optional)

1 Wash the rice in several changes of cold water until it runs clear. Place the water, coconut milk, salt and sugar in a heavy-bottomed saucepan.

2 Add the rice, cover, and bring to a boil. Reduce the heat to low and simmer for about 15–20 minutes, or until the rice is tender to the bite and cooked through.

3 Turn off the heat and allow the rice to rest in the saucepan for about 5–10 minutes.

4 Fluff up the rice with chopsticks before serving.

Pineapple Fried Rice

This dish is ideal to prepare for a special occasion meal. Served in the pineapple skin shells, it is certain to be the talking point of the dinner.

INGREDIENTS

Serves 4–6

1 pineapple
2 tablespoons vegetable oil
1 small onion, finely chopped
2 green chilies, seeded and chopped
8 ounces lean pork, cut into
small dice
4 ounces cooked shelled shrimp
3–4 cups cooked cold rice
½ cup roasted cashews
2 scallions, chopped
2 tablespoons fish sauce
1 tablespoon soy sauce
10–12 mint leaves, 2 red chilies, sliced,
and 1 green chili, sliced, to garnish

1 Cut the pineapple in half lengthwise and remove the flesh from both halves by cutting around inside the skin. Reserve the skin shells. You need 4 ounces of fruit, chopped finely (keep the rest for a dessert).

--- COOK'S TIP ---

When buying a pineapple, look for a sweet-smelling fruit with an even brownish-yellow skin. To test for ripeness, tap the base – a dull sound indicates that the fruit is ripe. The flesh should also give slightly when pressed.

2 Heat the oil in a wok or large frying pan. Add the onion and chilies and fry for about 3–5 minutes, until softened. Add the pork and cook until it is brown on all sides.

3 Stir in the shrimp and rice and toss well together. Continue to stir-fry until the rice is thoroughly heated.

4 Add the chopped pineapple, cashews and scallions. Season with fish sauce and soy sauce.

5 Spoon into the pineapple skin shells. Garnish with shredded mint leaves and red and green chilies.

Rice Porridge with Chicken

This dish is often served as sustaining breakfast fare. It can be served simply, with just the chicken stirred into it. Hearty eaters will relish helpings of porridge drizzled with a little soy sauce, with strips of chicken, shrimp, garlic and strips of fresh chili, topped with a lightly fried egg and garnished with celery leaves and fried onion.

INGREDIENTS

Serves 6

2¼ pounds chicken, cut into 4 pieces, or 4 chicken quarters
7½ cups water
1 large onion, quartered
1-inch piece fresh ginger, halved and bruised
12 ounces Thai fragrant rice, rinsed
salt and freshly ground black pepper
cooked peeled shrimp, strips of fresh chili, deep-fried onion and celery leaves, to garnish (optional)

1 Place the chicken pieces in a large saucepan with the water, onion and ginger. Season with salt and pepper, bring to a boil and simmer for 45–50 minutes, until the chicken is tender. Remove the chicken from the pan and reserve the broth. Remove the skin from the chicken pieces. Cut the meat from the bones and then into bite-sized pieces.

2 Strain and measure the reserved chicken broth. Increase the quantity to 7½ cups with water and transfer to a clean saucepan.

3 Add the rice to the broth and bring to a boil, stirring constantly. Lower the heat and simmer gently for 20 minutes. Stir, cover and cook for another 20 minutes, stirring from time to time, until the rice is soft.

4 Stir the chicken pieces into the porridge and heat through for 5 minutes. Serve as it is or with any of the garnishes suggested.

Spicy Peanut Rice Cakes

Serve these spicy Indonesian rice cakes with a crisp green salad and a dipping sauce, such as Hot Tomato Sambal.

INGREDIENTS

Makes 16

1 garlic clove, crushed
½-inch piece fresh ginger, finely chopped
¼ teaspoon ground turmeric
1 teaspoon sugar
½ teaspoon salt
1 teaspoon chili sauce
2 teaspoons fish sauce or soy sauce
2 tablespoons chopped fresh cilantro
juice of ½ lime
generous ½ cup long-grain rice, cooked
¾ cup raw peanuts, chopped
vegetable oil, for deep-frying

1 Pound together the garlic, ginger and turmeric in a mortar with a pestle or in a food processor. Add the sugar, salt, chili sauce, fish or soy sauce, cilantro and lime juice.

2 Add about ¼ cup of the cooked rice and pound until smooth and sticky. Stir the mixture into the remaining rice and mix well. With wet hands, shape 16 thumb-sized balls.

3 Spread the chopped peanuts out on a plate and roll the balls in them to coat evenly. Set aside.

4 Heat the oil in a preheated wok or deep frying pan. Deep-fry the rice cakes, three at a time, until crisp and golden. Remove and drain on paper towels. Serve immediately.

DESSERTS

*Surprise the family with something
completely different with these melt-in-
the-mouth dessert recipes collected from
all over China and the rest of Asia.
Exotic Fruit Salad from Vietnam tastes
just as wonderful—and refreshing—as it
looks. Old or young, few can resist the
delicious little Japanese Sweet Potato
and Chestnut Candies. Thailand offers
an intriguing variation on an
international favorite with Steamed
Coconut Custard, and the combination
of crisp batter and soft, warm fruit in
Indonesian Deep-fried Bananas is quite
simply magical.*

Chinese Fruit Salad

For an unusual fruit salad with
an Asian flavor, try this mixture
of fruits in a tangy lime and
lychee syrup, topped with a
light sprinkling of toasted
sesame seeds.

INGREDIENTS

Serves 4
½ cup superfine sugar
1¼ cups water
thinly pared rind and juice of 1 lime
1 can (14 ounces) lychees in syrup
1 ripe mango, peeled, pitted and sliced
1 eating apple, cored and sliced
2 bananas, chopped
1 star fruit, sliced (optional)
1 teaspoon sesame seeds, toasted

1 Place the sugar in a saucepan with
the water and the lime rind. Heat
gently until the sugar dissolves, then
increase the heat and boil gently for
about 7–8 minutes. Remove from the
heat and set aside to cool.

2 Drain the lychees and reserve the
juice. Pour the juice into the
cooled lime syrup with the lime juice.
Place all the prepared fruit in a bowl
and pour the lime and lychee syrup
over it. Chill for about 1 hour. Just
before serving, sprinkle with toasted
sesame seeds.

--- COOK'S TIP ---

To prepare a mango, cut through the fruit
lengthwise, about ½ inch either side of the
center. Then, using a sharp knife, cut the
flesh from the central piece from the pit.
Make even crisscross cuts in the flesh of
both side pieces. Hold one side piece in
both hands, bend it almost inside out and
remove the cubes of flesh with a spoon.
Repeat with the other side piece.

Sweet Potato and Chestnut Candies

It is customary in Japan to offer special bean-paste candies with tea. The candies tend to be very sweet by themselves, but contrast well with Japanese green tea. They also make an unusual dessert at the end of a special evening meal.

INGREDIENTS

Makes 18
1 pound sweet potatoes, chopped
¼ teaspoon salt
2 egg yolks
1 cup sugar
4 tablespoons water
5 tablespoons rice flour or
  all-purpose flour
1 teaspoon orange-flower or rose water
  (optional)
1 can (7 ounces) chestnuts in heavy
  syrup, drained
superfine sugar, for dusting
2 strips candied angelica
2 teaspoons plum or apricot preserves
3–4 drops red food coloring

1 Place the sweet potatoes in a heavy saucepan, cover with cold water and add the salt. Bring to a boil and simmer for 20–25 minutes, until the sweet potatoes are tender. Drain and return to the pan. Mash until smooth or rub through a wire sieve. Place the egg yolks, sugar and water in a bowl, then mix in the flour and orange-flower or rose water, if using. Add the sweet potato purée and stir over a pan of simmering water for 3–4 minutes. Transfer the paste to a tray and let cool.

2 To shape the paste, place 2 teaspoons of the mixture in the center of a wet cotton napkin. Enclose the paste in the napkin and twist into a nut shape. Repeat. Make sure the napkin is wet, or the mixture will stick to it.

3 To prepare the chestnuts, rinse off the syrup and dry well. Roll the chestnuts in superfine sugar and decorate with strips of angelica. To finish the sweet potato candies, color the plum or apricot preserves with red food coloring and decorate each candy with a spot of color.

COOK'S TIP

Sugar-coated chestnuts will keep for up to five days in a sealed container at room temperature. Store sweet potato candies in a sealed container in the refrigerator.

Thin Pancakes

Thin pancakes are not too difficult to make, but quite a lot of practice and patience are needed to achieve the perfect result. Nowadays, even restaurants buy frozen, ready-made ones from Chinese supermarkets. If you decide to use ready-made pancakes, or are reheating home-made ones, steam them for about five minutes, or microwave on high for one to two minutes.

INGREDIENTS

Makes 24–30
4 cups all-purpose flour, plus extra for
  dusting
about 1¼ cups boiling water
1 teaspoon vegetable oil

1 Sift the flour into a mixing bowl, then pour in the boiling water very gently, stirring as you pour. Mix with the oil and knead the mixture into a firm dough. Cover with a damp cloth and let stand for about 30 minutes.

2 Lightly dust a work surface with flour. Knead the dough for 5–8 minutes, or until smooth, then divide it into three equal portions. Roll out each portion into a long "sausage," cut each into eight to ten pieces and roll each into a ball. Using the palm of your hand, press each piece into a flat pancake. With a rolling pin, gently roll each into a 6-inch circle.

3 Heat an ungreased frying pan until hot, then reduce the heat to low and place the pancakes, one at a time, in the pan. Remove the pancakes when small brown spots appear on the underside. Keep under a damp cloth until all the pancakes are cooked.

Red Bean Paste Pancakes

If you are unable to find red bean paste, sweetened chestnut purée or mashed dates are possible substitutes.

INGREDIENTS

Serves 4
about 8 tablespoons sweetened red
  bean paste
8 Thin Pancakes
2–3 tablespoons vegetable oil
granulated or superfine sugar, to serve

1 Spread about 1 tablespoon of the red bean paste over about three-quarters of each pancake, then roll the pancake over three or four times.

2 Heat the oil in a preheated wok or frying pan and fry the pancake rolls until golden brown, turning once.

3 Cut each pancake roll into three or four pieces and sprinkle with sugar to serve.

Almond Curd Junket

Also known as almond float, this
dessert is usually made with agar
or isinglass, although gelatin can
also be used.

INGREDIENTS

Serves 4–6
¼ ounce agar or 1 ounce gelatin
    powder
about 2½ cups water
4 tablespoons superfine sugar
1¼ cups milk
1 teaspoon almond extract
fresh or canned mixed fruit salad with
    syrup, to serve

1 In a saucepan, dissolve the agar
in about half the water over gentle
heat. This will take at least 10 minutes.
(If using gelatin, follow the package
instructions.)

2 In a separate saucepan, dissolve the
sugar in the remaining water over
medium heat. Add the milk and the
almond extract, blending well. Do not
allow the mixture to boil.

3 Mix the milk and sugar with the agar
or gelatin mixture in a serving
bowl. When cool, place in the
refrigerator for 2–3 hours to set.

4 To serve, cut the junket into small
cubes and spoon into a serving dish
or into individual bowls. Pour the fruit
salad, with the syrup, over the junket
and serve.

Stewed Pumpkin in Coconut Cream

Stewed fruit is a popular dessert in Thailand. Use the firm-textured Japanese kabocha pumpkin for this dish, if you can. Bananas and melons can also be prepared in this way and you can even stew corn kernels or dried beans, such as mung beans and black beans, in coconut milk.

INGREDIENTS

Serves 4–6
2¼ pounds kabocha pumpkin
3 cups unsweetened coconut milk
scant 1 cup sugar
pinch of salt
pumpkin seed kernels, toasted, and
   mint sprigs, to decorate

1 Wash the pumpkin skin and cut off most of it. Scoop out the seeds.

COOK'S TIP

Any pumpkin can be used for this dessert, as long as it has a firm texture. Jamaican or New Zealand varieties both make good alternatives to kabocha pumpkin.

2 Using a sharp knife cut the flesh into pieces about 2 inches long and ¼ inch thick.

3 In a saucepan, bring the coconut milk, sugar and salt to a boil.

4 Add the pumpkin and simmer for 10–15 minutes, until the pumpkin is tender. Serve warm. Decorate each serving with a mint sprig and a few toasted pumpkin seed kernels

Celebration Cake

This mouthwatering cake is made from fragrant Thai rice covered with a tangy cream. Top with fresh berries or pipe on a greeting in melted chocolate.

INGREDIENTS

Serves 8–10
generous 1 cup Thai fragrant or
    jasmine rice
4 cups milk
generous ½ cup superfine sugar
2 bay leaves
6 cardamom pods, crushed open
1¼ cups heavy cream
6 eggs, separated

For the topping

1¼ cups heavy cream
scant 1 cup quark
1 teaspoon vanilla extract
grated rind of 1 lemon
soft berries and sliced star or kiwi
    fruits, to decorate

1 Grease and line a deep 10-inch round cake pan. Boil the rice in unsalted water for 3 minutes, then drain well.

COOK'S TIP

If you prefer something simpler, turn the cake out and top with sliced fruits or a lovely tumble of berries and pitted cherries. Serve the topping separately, thinning it down slightly with a little milk.

2 Return the rice to the pan with the milk, a generous ½ cup of the sugar, the bay leaves and the cardamom. Bring to a boil, then lower the heat and simmer the mixture for 20 minutes, stirring occasionally.

3 Allow the mixture to cool, then remove the bay leaves and any cardamom husks. Transfer to a large bowl. Beat in the cream and then the egg yolks.

4 Whisk the egg whites until they form soft peaks and fold into the rice mixture. Spoon into the prepared pan and bake in a preheated oven at 350°F for 45–50 minutes, until risen and golden brown. The center should be slightly wobbly—it will firm up as it cools.

5 Chill overnight in the pan. Turn out onto a large serving plate. Whip the heavy cream until stiff, then mix in the quark, vanilla extract, lemon rind and remaining sugar.

6 Cover the top and sides of the cake with the cream, swirling it attractively. Decorate with soft berries and sliced star or kiwi fruits.

Steamed Coconut Custard

Srikaya is a very popular dessert that turns up all over South-east Asia, rather as crème caramel is found all over Europe and the Americas.

INGREDIENTS

Serves 8
14-fluid ounce can coconut milk
5 tablespoons water
1 ounce sugar
3 eggs, beaten
1 ounce cellophane noodles, soaked in warm water for 5 minutes
4 ripe bananas or plantains, peeled and cut in small pieces
ꞁꞁꞁꞁ

vanilla ice cream, to serve (optional)

1 Stir the coconut milk, water and sugar into the beaten eggs and whisk well together.

2 Strain into a 7½-cup heatproof soufflé dish.

3 Drain the noodles well and cut them into small pieces with scissors. Stir the noodles into the coconut milk mixture, together with the chopped bananas or plantains. Stir in a pinch of salt.

4 Cover the dish with foil and place in a steamer for about 1 hour, or until set. Test by inserting a thin, small knife or skewer into the center. Serve hot or cold, on its own or topped with vanilla ice cream.

Date and Walnut Crisps

Try this sweet version of fried wontons; they make a truly scrumptious snack or dessert.

INGREDIENTS

Makes 15

25–30 dried dates, pitted
½ cup walnuts
2 tablespoons light brown sugar
pinch of ground cinnamon
30 wonton wrappers
1 egg, beaten
oil, for deep-frying
fresh mint sprigs, to decorate
confectioners' sugar, for dusting

1 Chop the dates and walnuts roughly. Place them in a bowl and add the sugar and cinnamon. Mix well.

2 Lay a wonton wrapper on a flat surface. Center a spoonful of the filling on the wrapper, brush the edges with beaten egg and cover with a second wrapper. Lightly press the edges together to seal. Make more filled wontons in the same way.

3 Heat the oil to 350°F in a wok or deep-fryer. Deep-fry the wontons, a few at a time, until golden. Do not crowd the pan. Remove the crisps with a slotted spoon and drain on paper towels. Serve warm, decorated with mint and dusted with confectioners' sugar.

Baked Rice Pudding, Thai-style

Black glutinous rice, also known as black sticky rice, has long black grains and a nutty taste similar to wild rice. This baked pudding has a distinct character and flavor all of its own.

INGREDIENTS

Serves 4–6

6 ounces white or black glutinous (sticky) rice
2 tablespoons light brown sugar
2 cups unsweetened coconut milk
1 cup water
3 eggs
2 tablespoons sugar

1 Combine the glutinous rice, brown sugar, half the coconut milk and all the water in a saucepan.

2 Bring to a boil and simmer for about 15–20 minutes, or until the rice has absorbed most of the liquid, stirring from time to time. Preheat the oven to 300°F.

3 Transfer the rice to one large ovenproof dish or divide it between individual ramekins. Mix together the eggs, remaining coconut milk and sugar in a bowl.

4 Strain and pour the mixture evenly over the par-cooked rice.

5 Place the dish in a baking pan. Pour in enough boiling water to come halfway up the sides of the dish.

6 Cover the dish with a piece of foil and bake in the oven for about 35 minutes to 1 hour, or until the custard is set. Serve warm or cold.

Mango with Sticky Rice

Everyone's favorite dessert. Mangoes, with their delicate fragrance, sweet and sour flavor and velvety flesh, blend especially well with coconut sticky rice. You need to start preparing this dish the day before.

INGREDIENTS

Serves 4

4 ounces glutinous (sticky) white rice
¾ cup thick unsweetened coconut milk
3 tablespoons sugar
pinch of salt
2 ripe mangoes
strips of lime rind, to decorate

1 Rinse the glutinous rice thoroughly in several changes of cold water, then let soak overnight in a bowl of fresh cold water.

2 Drain and spread the rice in an even layer in a steamer lined with cheesecloth. Cover and steam for about 20 minutes, or until the grains of rice are tender.

3 Meanwhile, reserve 3 tablespoons of the top of the coconut milk and combine the rest with the sugar and salt in a saucepan. Bring to a boil, stirring until the sugar dissolves, then pour into a bowl and let cool a little.

4 Turn the rice into a bowl and pour over the coconut mixture. Stir, then let stand for about 10–15 minutes.

5 Peel the mangoes and cut the flesh into slices. Place on top of the rice and drizzle over the reserved coconut milk. Decorate with strips of lime rind.

Sugar Bread Rolls

These delicious sweet rolls reveal the influence of Spain on the cooking of the Philippines. They make an unusual end to a special meal.

INGREDIENTS

Makes 10

3 cups stone-ground flour
1 teaspoon salt
1 tablespoon superfine sugar
1 teaspoon dried yeast
⅔ cup hot water
3 egg yolks
4 tablespoons unsalted butter, softened
¼ cup Cheddar cheese, grated
2 tablespoons melted unsalted butter
generous ¼ cup sugar

1 Sift the flour, salt and superfine sugar into a food processor fitted with a dough blade or the bowl of an electric mixer fitted with a dough hook. Make a well in the center. Dissolve the yeast in the hot water and pour into the well. Add the egg yolks and let sit until bubbles appear on the surface of the liquid.

2 Mix the ingredients for 30–45 seconds to form a firm dough. Add the softened butter and knead for 2–3 minutes in a food processor, or for 4–5 minutes with an electric mixer, until smooth. Turn the dough out into a floured bowl, cover and leave in a warm place to rise until doubled in volume.

3 Turn the dough out onto a lightly floured surface and divide it into ten pieces. Spread the grated cheese over the surface. Roll each of the dough pieces into 5-inch lengths, incorporating the cheese as you do so. Coil into snail shapes and place on a lightly greased high-sided baking sheet measuring 12 x 8 inches.

4 Cover the sheet with a loose-fitting plastic bag and leave in a warm place for 45 minutes, or until the dough has doubled in volume. Bake in a preheated oven at 375°F for 20–25 minutes. Brush with the melted butter, sprinkle with the sugar and let cool. Separate the rolls before serving.

Exotic Fruit Salad

A variety of fruits can be used
for this Vietnamese dessert,
depending on what is available.
Look for mandarin oranges, star
fruit, papaya and passion fruit.

INGREDIENTS

Serves 4–6
scant ½ cup sugar
1¼ cups water
2 tablespoons Canton ginger syrup
2 pieces star anise
1-inch piece cinnamon stick
1 clove
juice of ½ lemon
2 fresh mint sprigs
1 mango
2 bananas, sliced
8 fresh or canned lychees
8 ounces strawberries, hulled and
    halved
2 pieces Canton ginger, cut into sticks
1 medium pineapple

1 Put the sugar, water, ginger syrup,
star anise, cinnamon, clove, lemon
juice and mint in a saucepan. Bring to a
boil and simmer for 3 minutes. Strain
into a bowl and set aside to cool.

2 Remove the top and bottom from
the mango, then remove the outer
skin. Stand the mango on one end and
remove the flesh in two pieces on
either side of the flat pit. Slice evenly
and add to the syrup. Add the bananas,
lychees, strawberries and ginger.

3 Cut the pineapple in half down the
center. Loosen the flesh with a
small serrated knife and remove to
form two boat shapes. Cut the flesh
into chunks and place in the syrup.

4 Spoon some of the fruit salad into
the pineapple halves and serve on a
large dish. There will be sufficient fruit
salad to refill the pineapple halves.

Black Glutinous Rice Pudding

This very unusual rice pudding, *Bubor Pulot Hitam,* which uses bruised fresh ginger root, is quite delicious. When cooked, black rice still retains its husk and has a nutty texture. Serve in small bowls, with a little coconut cream poured over each helping.

INGREDIENTS

Serves 6
4 ounces black glutinous rice
2 cups water
½ inch fresh ginger root, peeled
  and bruised
⅛ cup dark brown sugar
¼ cup superfine sugar
1¼ cups coconut milk
  or cream, to serve

1 Put the rice in a strainer and rinse well under cold running water. Drain and put in a large pan, with the water. Bring to a boil and stir to prevent the rice from settling on the bottom of the pan. Cover and cook for about 30 minutes.

2 Add the ginger and the brown and superfine sugars. Cook for about 15 minutes more, adding a little more water if necessary, until the rice is cooked and like porridge. Remove the ginger and serve warm, in bowls, topped with coconut milk or cream.

Deep-fried Bananas

Known as *Pisang Goreng,* these delicious deep-fried bananas should be cooked at the last minute, so that the outer crust of batter is crisp in texture and the banana is soft and warm inside.

INGREDIENTS

Serves 8
4 ounces self-rising flour
⅜ cup rice flour
½ teaspoon salt
1 cup water
finely grated lime rind (optional)
8 small bananas
oil for deep-frying
sugar and 1 lime, cut in wedges,
  to serve

1 Sift both the flours and the salt together into a bowl. Add just enough water to make a smooth, coating batter. Mix well, then add the lime rind, if using.

2 Peel the bananas and dip them into the batter two or three times.

3 Heat the oil to 375°F or when a cube of day-old bread browns in 30 seconds. Deep-fry the batter-coated bananas until crisp and golden. Drain and serve hot, dredged with sugar and with the lime wedges to squeeze over the bananas.

Thai Coconut Custard

This traditional dish can be baked or steamed, and is often served with sweet sticky rice and a selection of fruit, such as mango and persimmons.

INGREDIENTS

Serves 4–6

4 eggs
6 tablespoons light brown sugar
1 cup unsweetened coconut milk
1 teaspoon vanilla, rose or
  jasmine extract
mint leaves and confectioner's sugar,
  to decorate

1 Preheat the oven to 300°F. Whisk the eggs and sugar in a bowl until they are smooth. Add the coconut milk and vanilla or other extract and blend well together.

2 Strain the mixture and pour into individual ramekins or a cake pan.

3 Stand the ramekins or pan in a roasting pan. Carefully fill the roasting pan with hot water to reach halfway up the outsides of the ramekins or cake pan.

4 Bake for about 35–40 minutes, or until the custards are set. Test with a fine skewer or toothpick.

5 Remove from the oven and cool. Turn out on to a plate, and serve with sliced fruit. Decorate with mint leaves and confectioner's sugar.

Apples and Raspberries in Rose Pouchong Syrup

This delightfully fragrant and quick-to-prepare Asian dessert couples the subtle flavors of apples and raspberries, both of which belong to the rose family, within an infusion of rose-scented tea.

INGREDIENTS

Serves 4
1 teaspoon rose pouchong tea
1 teaspoon rose water (optional)
¼ cup sugar
1 teaspoon lemon juice
5 apples
1½ cups fresh raspberries

1 Warm a large teapot. Add the rose pouchong tea and 3¾ cups of boiling water together with the rose water, if using. Allow to stand and infuse for 4 minutes.

2 Measure the sugar and lemon juice into a stainless steel saucepan. Strain in the tea and stir to dissolve the sugar.

3 Peel and core the apples, then cut into quarters.

4 Poach the apples in the syrup for about 5 minutes.

5 Transfer the apples and syrup to a large metal baking sheet and let cool to room temperature.

6 Pour the cooled apples and syrup into a bowl, add the raspberries and mix to combine. Spoon into individual dishes or bowls and serve immediately.

SAUCES AND SAMBALS

Dipping sauces are often served with spring rolls, meat, fish, salads and vegetables. Sometimes, they provide a cooling or creamy contrast to hot spiced dishes. More often, they add piquancy and may be very fiery. Sambals, pungent relishes that originated in southern India, are now served throughout South-east Asia, particularly in Indonesia. They may contain chicken or seafood and a mixture of vegetables, sometimes making a quite substantial accompaniment. Whether raw or cooked, they are invariably very hot.

Hot Chili and Garlic Dipping Sauce

Sambals are placed on the table as a condiment and are used mainly for dipping meat and fish in Indonesia. They are quite strong and should be used sparingly.

INGREDIENTS

Makes ½ cup
1 garlic clove, crushed
2 small fresh red chilies, seeded and
   finely chopped
2 teaspoons sugar
1 teaspoon tamarind sauce
4 tablespoons soy sauce
juice of ½ lime

1 Pound the garlic, chilies and sugar until smooth in a mortar with a pestle. Alternatively, grind them together in a food processor.

2 Add the tamarind sauce, soy sauce and lime juice. Stir well.

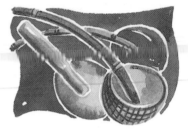

Hot Tomato Sambal

This is a particularly popular sambal and goes well with most kinds of meat and poultry.

INGREDIENTS

Makes ½ cup
3 ripe tomatoes
½ teaspoon salt
1 teaspoon chili sauce
4 tablespoons fish sauce or soy sauce
1 tablespoon chopped fresh cilantro

1 Place the tomatoes in a bowl and cover with boiling water for 30 seconds to loosen their skins. Remove the skins, halve and seed the tomatoes, then chop finely.

2 Place the chopped tomatoes in a bowl and mix with the salt, chili sauce, fish sauce or soy sauce and cilantro.

COOK'S TIP

If you like really fiery food, you can add 1 or even 2 seeded and finely chopped fresh red chilies.

Sambal Goreng

Traditional flavorings for this dish are fine strips of calves' liver, chicken livers, green beans or hard-boiled eggs. A westernized version is shown here.

INGREDIENTS

Makes 3¼ cups

1 teaspoon shrimp paste
2 onions, quartered
2 garlic cloves, crushed
1 inch fresh *laos*, peeled and sliced
2 teaspoons Chili Sambal or 2 fresh red chilies, seeded and sliced
¼ teaspoon salt
2 tablespoons oil
3 tablespoons tomato paste
2½ cups broth or water
4 tablespoons tamarind juice
pinch sugar
3 tablespoons coconut milk or cream

1 Grind the shrimp paste, with the onions and garlic, to a paste in a food processor or with a mortar and pestle. Add the *laos*, Chili Sambal or sliced chilies and salt. Process or pound to a fine paste.

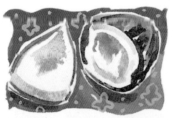

2 Fry the paste in hot oil for 2 minutes, without browning, until the mixture gives off a rich aroma.

3 Add the tomato paste and the broth or water and cook for about 10 minutes. Add 12 ounces cooked chicken pieces and 2 ounces cooked and sliced French beans, or one of the flavoring variations below, to half the quantity of the sauce. Cook in the sauce for 3–4 minutes, then stir in the tamarind juice, sugar and coconut milk or cream at the last minute, before tasting and serving.

VARIATIONS

Tomato *Sambal Goreng* – Add 1 pound of peeled, seeded and coarsely chopped tomatoes, before the broth.

Shrimp *Sambal Goreng* – Add 12 ounces cooked, peeled shrimp and 1 green bell pepper, seeded and chopped.

Egg *Sambal Goreng* – Add 3 or 4 hard-boiled eggs, shelled and chopped, and 2 tomatoes, peeled, seeded and chopped.

Mixed Vegetable Pickle

If you can obtain fresh turmeric, it makes such a difference to the color and appearance of *Acar Campur*. You can use almost any vegetable, bearing in mind that you need a balance of textures, flavors and colors.

INGREDIENTS

Makes 2–3 11-ounce jars
1 fresh red chili, seeded and sliced
1 onion, quartered
2 garlic cloves, crushed
½ teaspoon shrimp paste
4 macadamia nuts or 8 almonds
1 inch fresh turmeric, peeled and
    sliced, or 1 teaspoon ground turmeric
7 tbsp sunflower oil
2 cups white vinegar
1 cup water
3–6 tablespoons granulated sugar
3 carrots
8 ounces green beans
1 small cauliflower
1 cucumber
8 ounces white cabbage
¾ cup dry-roasted peanuts,
    roughly crushed
salt

1 Place the chili, onion, garlic, shrimp paste, nuts and turmeric in a food processor and blend to a paste, or pound in a mortar with a pestle.

2 Heat the oil and stir-fry the paste to release the aroma. Add the vinegar, water, sugar and salt. Bring to a boil. Simmer for 10 minutes.

3 Cut the carrots into flower shapes. Cut the green beans into short, neat lengths. Separate the cauliflower into neat, bite-size florets. Peel and seed the cucumber and cut the flesh in neat, bite-size pieces. Cut the cabbage in neat, bite-size pieces.

4 Blanch each vegetable separately, in a large pan of boiling water, for 1 minute. Transfer to a colander and rinse with cold water, to halt the cooking. Drain well.

--- COOK'S TIP ---

This pickle is even better if you make it a few days ahead.

5 Add the vegetables to the sauce. Slowly bring to a boil and allow to cook for 5–10 minutes. Do not overcook – the vegetables should still be crunchy.

6 Add the peanuts and cool. Spoon into clean jars with lids.

Sweet-and-Sour Ginger Sambal

This sambal is especially delicious with fish, chicken or pork—but beware, it is extremely hot.

INGREDIENTS

Makes 6 tablespoons
4–5 small fresh red chilies, seeded and chopped
2 shallots or 1 small onion, chopped
2 garlic cloves
¼-inch fresh ginger
2 tablespoons sugar
¼ teaspoon salt
3 tablespoons rice vinegar or white wine vinegar

1 Pound together the chilies and shallots or onion in a mortar with a pestle. Alternatively, grind them in a food processor.

2 Add the garlic, ginger, sugar and salt and continue to pound or grind until smooth. Stir in the vinegar and mix well.

--- COOK'S TIP ---

This sambal can be stored for up to a week in a screw-top jar in the refrigerator.

Satay Sauce

There are many versions of this tasty peanut sauce. This one is very speedy and it tastes delicious drizzled over grilled or barbecued skewers of chicken. For parties, spear chunks of chicken with toothpicks and arrange around a bowl of warm satay sauce.

INGREDIENTS

Serves 4
scant 1 cup coconut cream
4 tablespoons crunchy peanut butter
1 teaspoon Worcestershire sauce
few drops of Tabasco sauce
fresh coconut, to garnish (optional)

1 Pour the coconut cream into a small saucepan and heat it gently over low heat for about 2 minutes.

2 Add the peanut butter and stir vigorously until the mixture is thoroughly blended. Continue to heat, but do not allow to boil.

3 Add the Worcestershire sauce and Tabasco sauce to taste. Pour into a serving bowl.

4 Use a potato peeler to shave thin strips from a piece of fresh coconut, if using. Scatter the coconut over the sauce and serve immediately.

Vietnamese Dipping Sauce

Serve this dip in a small bowl as
an accompaniment to spring rolls
or meat dishes.

INGREDIENTS

Makes ⅔ cup
1–2 small fresh red chilies, seeded and
  finely chopped
1 garlic clove, crushed
1 tablespoon roasted peanuts
4 tablespoons coconut milk
2 tablespoons fish sauce
juice of 1 lime
2 teaspoons sugar
1 teaspoon chopped fresh cilantro

1 Pound the chili or chilies with the
garlic in a mortar with a pestle.

2 Add the peanuts and pound until
crushed. Add the coconut milk,
fish sauce, lime juice, sugar and cilantro.
Mix well.

Thai Dipping Sauce

Nam prik is the most common
dipping sauce in Thailand. It has
a fiery strength, so use it with
caution.

INGREDIENTS

Makes ½ cup
1 tablespoon vegetable oil
½-inch square shrimp paste or
  1 tablespoon fish sauce
2 garlic cloves, finely sliced
¾-inch piece fresh ginger, finely
  chopped
3 small fresh red chilies, seeded
  and chopped
1 tablespoon finely chopped cilantro
  root or stem
4 teaspoons sugar
3 tablespoons dark soy sauce
juice of ½ lime

1 Heat the vegetable oil in a
preheated wok. Add the shrimp
paste or fish sauce, garlic, ginger and
chilies and stir-fry for 1–2 minutes,
until softened, but not colored.

2 Remove from the heat and add the
chopped cilantro, sugar, soy sauce
and lime juice.

COOK'S TIP

Thai Dipping Sauce will keep for
up to 10 days in a screw-top jar in
the refrigerator.

Hoisin Dip

This speedy dip needs no cooking and can be made in just a few minutes—it tastes great with Mini Spring Rolls or shrimp crackers.

INGREDIENTS

Serves 4

4 scallions
1½-inch piece fresh ginger
2 fresh red chilies
2 garlic cloves
4 tablespoons hoisin sauce
½ cup tomato paste
1 teaspoon sesame oil (optional)

1 Trim off and discard the green ends of the scallions. Slice the white parts very thinly.

2 Peel and finely chop the ginger.

3 Halve and seed the chilies. Slice finely. Finely chop the garlic.

4 Stir together the hoisin sauce, tomato paste, scallions, ginger, chilies, garlic and sesame oil, if using. Serve within 1 hour.

Cucumber Sambal

This sauce has a piquant flavor and does not have the heat of chilies found in other sambals.

INGREDIENTS

Makes ²⁄₃ cup

1 garlic clove, crushed
1 teaspoon fennel seeds
2 teaspoons sugar
½ teaspoon salt
2 shallots or 1 small onion, finely sliced
½ cup rice or white wine vinegar
¼ cucumber, finely diced

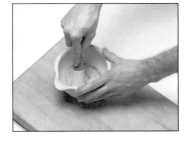

1 Pound together the garlic, fennel seeds, sugar and salt in a mortar with a pestle. Alternatively, grind them together in a food processor.

2 Stir in the shallots or onion, vinegar and cucumber and set aside for at least 6 hours to allow the flavors to combine.

INDEX